the survivor songbook 2

The words of all the songs in this publication are covered by the Church Copyright Licence

United Kingdom: CCL (EUROPE), PO Box 1339, Eastbourne, East Sussex, BN21 1AD, UK

United States: CCLI, 17201 NE Sacramento Street, Portland, Oregon 97230, USA

Australasia: CCL Asia Pacific Pty Ltd, PO Box 6644, Baulkham Hills Business Centre, NSW 2153, Australia

Africa: CCL Africa Ltd, PO Box 2347, Durbanville 7551, South Africa

ISBN 1 84291 112 0

Compiled by Les Moir & Matt Weeks

CD- Rom compilation by Chris Tice

Music Setting by David Ball davidoxon@aol.com

Music Arrangers - Matt Weeks, Andrew Philip, Martin Cooper, Mike Sandeman, Chris Norton, Cath Burton, Steve Harding, Nigel Hemming, Simon Fenner, David Ball, Craig Mcleish and Lizzie Haye

The Unquenchable Worshipper published by Survivor

Thanks to Vince Marsicano at Worship Together EMI, George Earey, Liselle Wilsnagh, Andrea Marden, Matt Weeks, Andrew Philip, Sue Lockhart and Rachael Cross

Cover Design Mike Thorpe

Printed in the United Kingdom by Halstan & Co Ltd, Amersham, Bucks for SURVIVOR, Lottbridge Drove, Eastbourne, East Sussex, BN23 6NT, UK

Contents

Father To The Fatherless

Paul Oakley

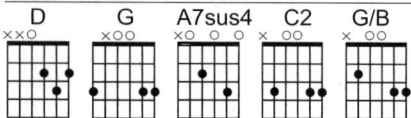

Capo 2

Verse 1:
   A7sus4 D   A7sus4 D
A Father to the fatherless
    G   A7sus4 D
My shelter from the storm
    A7sus4 D   A7sus4 D
My fountain in the wilderness
    G   A7sus4 D
My refuge and my rock
         G   D
High King of love, God of all grace
         G   A7sus4
Perfect in power and strong to save
         D   A7sus4 D
You have become my all in all
    G   A7sus4 D
My comfort and my peace

Link:
C2 G/B C2 G/B A7sus4 D A7sus4 D

Verse 2:
A lover to the loveless
Defender of the weak
The healer of all brokenness
Restorer of my dreams
High King of love, God of all grace
Perfect in power and strong to save
You have become my all in all
My comfort and my peace

Link:
C2 G/B C2 G/B A7sus4 D A7sus4 D

Verse 3:
My substitute, my sacrifice
My perfect spotless lamb
My risen Lord, my gift of life
My Saviour and my friend
High King of love, God of all grace
Perfect in power and strong to save
You have become my righteousness
My glory and my song

Link:
C2 G/B C2 G/B A7sus4 D A7sus4 D

Taken from
BE LIFTED UP
Paul Oakley
SURCD085

Father To The Fatherless

Paul Oakley

E	A	Bsus4	D	A/C#

Verse 1:
```
  Bsus4 E     Bsus4 E
A Father to the fatherless
     A     Bsus4     E
My shelter from the storm
  Bsus4   E    Bsus4 E
My fountain in the wilderness
     A     Bsus4  E
My refuge and my rock
               A              E
High King of love, God of all grace
          A                   Bsus4
Perfect in power and strong to save
               E      Bsus4 E
You have become my all  in  all
     A     Bsus4 E
My comfort and my peace
```

Link:
D A/C# D A/C# Bsus4 E Bsus4 E

Verse 2:
A lover to the loveless
Defender of the weak
The healer of all brokenness
Restorer of my dreams
High King of love, God of all grace
Perfect in power and strong to save
You have become my all in all
My comfort and my peace

Link:
D A/C# D A/C# Bsus4 E Bsus4 E

Verse 3:
My substitute, my sacrifice
My perfect spotless lamb
My risen Lord, my gift of life
My Saviour and my friend
High King of love, God of all grace
Perfect in power and strong to save
You have become my righteousness
My glory and my song

Link:
D A/C# D A/C# Bsus4 E Bsus4 E

Taken from
BE LIFTED UP
Paul Oakley
SURCD085

A HUMBLE HEART

God Of Creation

G	Em7	F	D	C2	G/B	Am7

Verse 1:
G   Em7
A humble heart and impassioned soul
   F   D
Are my offering of worship
G   Em7
  Reaching out and declaring love
 F   D
To my King of all

Pre-Chorus:
     C2   G/B
Here I am O Lord
    D   Em7
My feet on holy ground
      C2   G/B   D
Heaven come as the earth lifts Your name, Your name

Chorus:
G   Em7
Jesus, God of creation
      F   D
Hear my voice rise up now and praise You
G   Em7
Saviour, King of the heavens
      F   D
My soul longs to see You reign
G   Em7
Jesus, now and forever
      F   D
You are God, let all things adore You
 Am7   D   C2   G
I lift my voice to You, God of creation

Verse 2:
You are more than all precious things
That man worships above You
A perfect Son as a sacrifice
Comes only through God

Taken from
SONGS OF HEAVEN
YFriday
YFCD02

A LOVE SO AMAZING

3

Love So Amazing

Paul Oakley

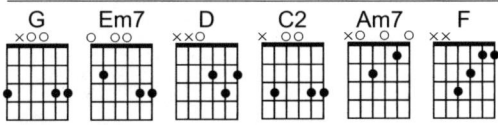

G   Em7   D   C2   Am7   F

Intro: G Em7 D C2 x2

Verse 1:
```
G                      Em7
  A love so amazing      has come to save me
C2                       G
  And this love changes everything
G                      Em7
  Father You found me,      Your goodness surrounds me
C2                  G     D
  I'm Your's for eternity
```

Chorus 1:
```
              G                        C2
And You will always be the King on the throne
              G                        C2
Now Your praise will always be on my tongue
        Em7                            C2       D  C2
No one else could do the things that You've done in my life
```

Verse 2:
Your ways are faithful, Your works are beautiful
Your word sets the captives free
Your hand upon me, heals and restores me
Your grace fills my every need

Chorus 2:
And You will always be the King on the throne
Now Your praise will always be on my tongue
No one else could do the things that You've done in my life
There's no greater love that's ever been shown
Now Your song in me just has to be sung
No one else could do the things that You've done in my life

Bridge:
```
Am7         C2          G
   You said if I follow You
Am7             C2          G        D
   I'll know the truth and do the things You do
Am7             C2             G
   Yours is the kingdom and the power
  Am7               F          D
Forever Lord You will always be my God
```

Taken from
BE LIFTED UP
Paul Oakley
SURCD085

Amazing   **Matt Redman**

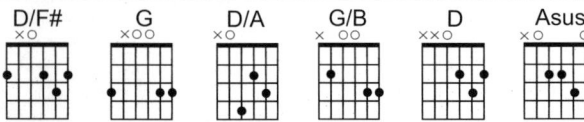

D/F#   G   D/A   G/B   D   Asus

Intro: D/F# G D/A G/B   x2

Verse 1:
D/F#   G
A love so undeserved
   D/A   G/B
A gift that's free You lavish on me
D/F#   G
A peace I could not earn
     D/A   G/B   D/F# G D/A G/B
And mercy for the freedom of my soul

Chorus:
D   G   D/A   G/B
That's what's so amazing about Your grace
D   G   D/A   G/B
That's what's so amazing about Your grace
      D/F#   G   D/A   G/B
Lord everyday You pour on me Your blessings of eternity
D   G   D/A   G
That's what's so amazing about Your grace

Verse 2:
Forgiveness runs so deep
Within your heart of loving kindness
And should a soul forget
The cross of Christ reminds us everyday

Link:
D/F# G Asus   x4

Bridge:
  D/F#   G
Freely I've received now freely to give
  D/A   G/B
Freely I've received now freely to give
  D/F#   G
Freely I've received now freely to give
D/A   G/B
Give my life to You

Taken from
WHERE ANGELS FEAR TO TREAD
Matt Redman
SURCD074

ABOVE ALL

Lenny LeBlanc & Paul Baloche

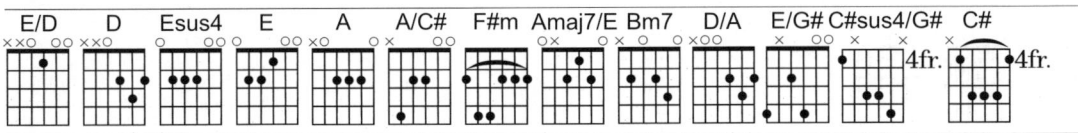

Verse 1:
      E/D D Esus4 E   A
Above all powers,   above all kings
 A/C#   E/D D   Esus4 E   A
Above all nature, and all created things
 A/C#   F#m   Amaj7/E   D A/C#
Above all wisdom and all the ways of man
Bm7   D/A   E/G#   A
You were here before the world began

Verse 2:
 A/C#   E/D D Esus4 E   A
Above all kingdoms,   above all thrones
 A/C#   E/D D   Esus4   E   A
Above all wonders the world has ever known
 A/C#   F#m   Amaj7/E   D   A/C#
Above all wealth and treasures of the earth
Bm7   D/A   C#sus4/G#   C#
There's no way to measure what Youre worth

Chorus:
A   Bm7 E/G#   A
Crucified,   laid behind the stone
    A   Bm7 E/G#   A
You lived to die, rejected and alone
E/G# F#m Amaj7/E   D
Like a rose trampled on the ground
A/C#   Bm7
   You took the fall
A/C#   D   Esus4
   And thought of me
E   A
Above all

Taken from
WORSHIP
Michael W Smith
602341002523

AFTER ALL THAT WE'VE BEEN THROUGH

Carry Me

Aaron Frith

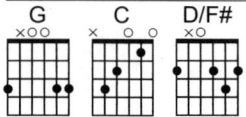

(Capo 4)

Verse 1:
```
B (G)                    E (C)          F#/A# (D/F#)
   After all that we've been through
                      B (G)
This journey carries on
                           E (C)         F#/A# (D/F#)
Through the laughter and the heartache
                      B (G)
Through the rain and sun
       E (C)            F#/A# (D/F#)
Why You've stuck with me
           B (G)
I'll never understand
             E (C)          F#/A# (D/F#)
Is grace in Your instincts?
                       B (G)
Because I keep falling into Your hands
```

Chorus:
```
             E (C)          F#/A# (D/F#)
You've carried me
                   B (G)
You've always carried me, Jesus
             E (C)          F#/A# (D/F#)
You've carried me
                   B (G)
You've always carried me
```

Verse 2:
I used to think I found You, but now I've realised I'm the fool
Because really You found me, You were on standby for my call
You laid down Your own life, and traded it for me
With blood You bought freedom, and gave it me for free

Verse 3:
I will be more popular, with You than my friends
Because You're the only reason I'm alive today

Taken from
BIOGRAPHY
Revelation Warehouse
SURCD079
and
ESCAPE by SABIO

ALL OF ME

Martyn Layzell & Mike Busbee

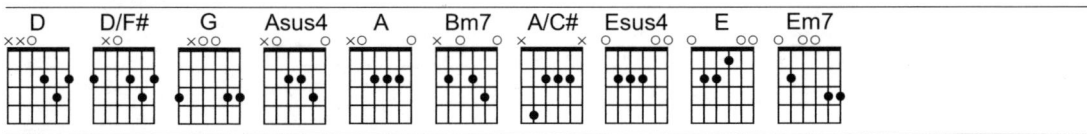

Verse 1:
```
D  D/F# G              D  D/F# G
All of  me, Jesus You have all  of me
                   D D/F# G
Nothing from You will I  keep
        Asus4     A
Now I am Yours
D  D/F# G              D  D/F# G
All of  me, Jesus You have all  of me
            D    D/F#   G
I will sing beneath Your wings
        Asus4     A
Now I am yours
```

Chorus:
```
    Bm7        Asus4
And I'm forever grateful
        G             D/F#
That You died upon the cross
    Bm7        Asus4
A never failing sacrifice
    G           A    A/C#
Declaring Your true love
    Bm7            Asus4
So through Your grace I give You
     G    D/F# Esus4  E
This living sacrifice
    Em7        Asus4
My offering of worship
    D  D/F#  G        D  D/F#  G
My life
```

Verse 2:
```
All of me, Jesus You have all of me
Everything to You I bring
Now I am Yours
All of me, Jesus You have all of me
I surrender as I sing
Now I am Yours
```

Optional Instrumental:
```
Bm7  Asus4  G  G      G  D/F#  Em7  Asus4  x4
```

Taken from
LOST IN WONDER
Martyn Layzell
SURCD076

ALL OF ME

Gareth Robinson

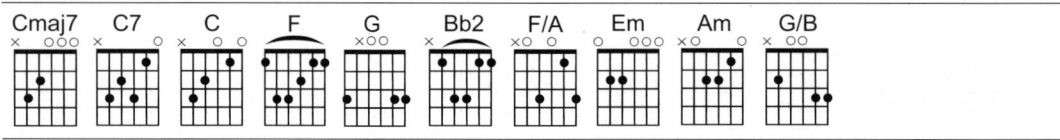

Verse 1:
```
     Cmaj7    C7
All of me
 C      F          G
All  of  me I give to You
  C    G      C    Bb2  F/A
Only You Jesus
       Cmaj7    C7
More of You
  C      F          G
More of You I long for
  C    G      C    Bb2  F/A  G
Only You Jesus
```


Chorus:
```
     C               Em
For this life I live for You
Am           Em
I truly worship You
Am           Em
All of my days, in every way
F  G  F/A   G/B
I  will praise You
C                       Em
In thought and word and deed
    Am                  Em
Powered by Your life in me
Am           Em
All of my days, in every way
F  G  F/A   G/B    C
I  will praise You Lord
```

Taken from YOU ALONE
Gareth Robinson
KMCD2494

Enough

A D/F# E D A/C# Bm7

Intro: A   D/F#   E   D   x2

Chorus:
```
      A     D/F#        E       D      A
All of You is more than enough for  all of me
D/F#      E       D      A
For every thirst and  every need
D/F#     E     D           A/C#
You satisfy me  with Your love
       D         E              A
And all I have in You is more than enough
```

Verse 1:
```
A        D     E     A/C#     D
  You are my supply, my breath of life
             Bm7              E
And still more awesome than I know
A        D     E           A/C#  D
  You are my reward, worth living for
             Bm7              E
And still more awesome than I know
```

Verse 2:
```
You're my sacrifice of greatest price
And still more awesome than I know
You're the coming King, You are everything
And still more awesome than I know
```

Bridge:
```
A          D    E
  More than all I want
           D   A/C#
More than all I need
D        E
  You are more than enough for me
A          D    E
  More than all I know
           D    A/C#
More than all I can see
D         E
  You are more than enough for me
```

Taken from NOT TO US
Chris Tomlin
SPD 38661

ALL THAT I WANT

Secret Place

Gareth Robinson & Dan Welberry

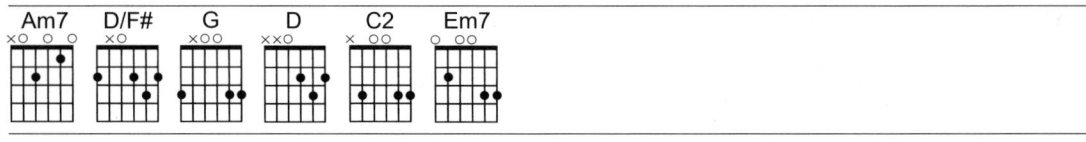

Am7   D/F#   G   D   C2   Em7

Verse 1:
```
Am7          D/F#
    All that I want is to be
Am7                D/F#
    Known as Your child and to
Am7              D/F#
    Speak of Your love and to
Am7              D/F#
    Move in Your power
```

Verse 2:
Jesus You are all I
Need in this world, and this
Friendship I've found is much
More than I deserve

Chorus:
```
G        D        C2      D
 I will seek You, here I'll find You
G        D          C2         D
In this place where You and I hide
G        D        C2          D
Here I'll love You, know You, trust You
C2                   D
    And I'll become one with You
```

Verse 3:
So I will give all I
Am to this cause just to
See You as King and to
Know You as Lord

Bridge:
```
Em7
     Let this secret place be the foundation of my life
Em7
     Let this secret place be the foundation of my life
```

Taken from
YOU ALONE
Gareth Robinson
KMCD2494

ALL THE KINGS WILL BOW

David Gate

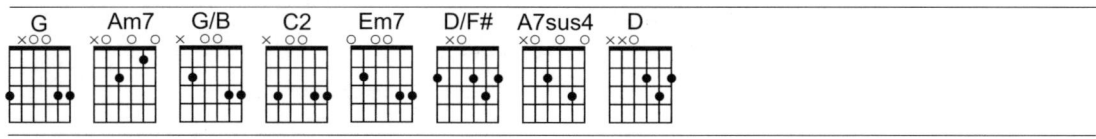

Verse 1:
```
             G      Am7  G/B
All the kings will bow
                      C2
And fall down at Your feet
                 Em7
The people of the earth
     D/F#           G
Will lay down their crowns
     A7sus4    C2
And lift up Your name
```

Pre-Chorus:
```
     Am7   G/B    C2        D
With angels and archangels singing
            Am7   G/B    C2   D
With the voice of heaven's choir bringing
Am7     G/B      C2     D     Am7  G/B
Songs of love that rise up to Your throne
```

Chorus:
```
C2     D       G
   You are who was and is
    D/F#
And is to come
Em7              C2
Jesus, Son of God        (repeat)
```

Verse 2:
```
We shall come and praise
And fall down at Your feet
In the presence of the Holy One
We'll fall onto our knees
```

Taken from
GLIMPSES OF GLORY
Soul Survivor Live 2002
SURCD082

ALL WHO ARE THIRSTY

Brenton Brown & Glenn Robertson

G   Bm7   C2   Am7   G/B   C/G

Verse 1:

          G
All who are thirsty
          Bm7
All who are weak
           C2
Come to the fountain
             Am7 G/B C2
Dip your heart in the stream of life
            G
Let the pain and the sorrow
          Bm7
Be washed away
            C2
In the waves of his mercy
        Am7 G/B C2
As deep cries out to deep

We sing...

Chorus:
  G   C/G   G   C2
Come Lord Je - sus come
  G   C/G   G   C2
Come Lord Je - sus come
  G   C/G   G   C2
Come Lord Je - sus come
  G   C/G   G   C2
Come Lord Je - sus come

Alt Chorus Lyrics:
Holy Spirit Come   x4

Taken from
COME NOW IS THE TIME TO WORSHIP
Vineyard Music UK
1995002

ALLELUIA

Agnus Dei

Michael W. Smith

A   Asus4   D/F#   E   D

Verse:
A   Asus4   A   Asus4
Alleluia
A   Asus4   A
Alleluia
        D/F#   A   Asus4   A   Asus4
For the Lord God Almighty reigns

A   Asus4   A   Asus4
Alleluia
A   Asus4   A
Alleluia
        D/F#   A   Asus4   A   Asus4
For the Lord God Almighty reigns
A   Asus4   A
Alleluia

A   Asus4   A   Asus4
Alleluia
A   Asus4   A
Alleluia

Chorus:
  A
Holy, Holy
                     E
Are You Lord God Almighty
            D
Worthy is the Lamb, worthy is the Lamb
         A
You are Holy, Holy
                     E
Are You Lord God Almighty
            D
Worthy is the Lamb, worthy is the Lamb
       A
Alleluia

Taken from
GLIMPSES OF GLORY
Soul Survivor Live 2002
SURCD082

ALMIGHTY GOD

Rhys Scott

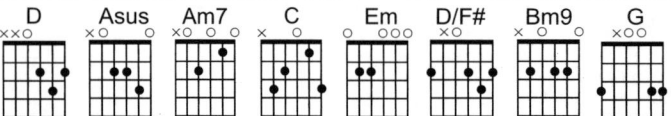

(Capo 3)

Verse 1:
```
        F (D)
Almighty God
  Csus (Asus)
Holy One
Cm7 (Am7)        Eb (C)
Who can stand before You?
          Csus (Asus)
Who can come?
          F (D)
Perfect Lamb
          Csus (Asus)
Who bore our sin
Cm7 (Am7)            Eb (C)
Who deserves such mercy
          Csus (Asus)
Gracious King?
```

Chorus:
```
   F (D)  Gm (Em)  F/A (D/F#)  Gm (Em)  Csus (Asus)
I come    to      Your      throne of  grace
                   F (D)
I'm standing in Christ
                 Gm (Em)   Csus (Asus)
I'm clothed in His righteous - ness
   Dm9 (Bm9)      Bb (G)
To know Your presence
Csus (Asus)       Dm9 (Bm9)
    To seek Your face
  Gm (Em)   Csus (Asus)
Father  I  delight
  Gm (Em)      F (D)
In Your embrace
```

Taken from DREAMS & VISIONS
Re:vive@Stoneleigh
SURCD059

AMAZING GRACE

John Newton, adapted by **Nathan Fellingham**

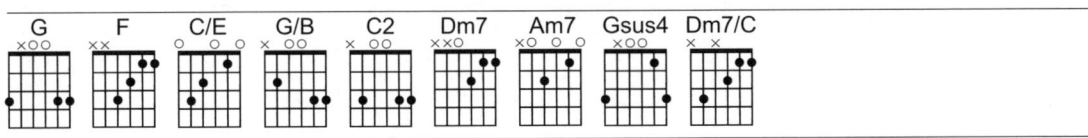

Verse 1:
```
G  F        C/E      G/B  C2  Dm7
   Amazing grace how sweet the sound
        Am7           G Gsus4 G Gsus4
That saved a wretch like me
G  F        C/E      G/B C2  Dm7
   I once was lost but now am found
        Am7         G  Gsus4  G
Was blind but now I see
```

Bridge:
```
Dm7  Dm7/C Gsus4  G  Gsus4  G
     Amazing love
Dm7       Dm7/C Gsus4  G
     Has come to me
```

Chorus:
```
          C2            F
I lift up my voice to the heavens
          C/E           F
Lift up my hands to the King
          Am7     G   C/E     F
And I cry 'hosanna, hosanna in the highest'
          C2        F
Jesus my Lord is exalted
          C/E    F
Far above every name
          Am7     G   C/E     F
And I cry 'hosanna, hosanna in the highest'
```

Verse 2:
'Twas grace that taught my heart to fear
And grace my fears relieved
How precious did that grace appear
The hour I first believed

Verse 3:
The Lord has promised good to me
His word my hope secures
He will my shield and portion be
As long as life endures

Taken from
CHOSEN FROM THE NATIONS
Stoneleigh Live Worship 2000
KMCD2288

(no capo)

Verse 1:
```
B          G#m        E              B
 And after all,    everything I once held dear
     F#        G#m      E
Just proved to be so vain
B          G#m           E              B
 To lose it all     and find a friend who's always near
        E        G#m      E
Could only be my gain
F#                                      E   B
  And when I think of what You've done for me
G#m          E            F#
   To bring me to the Father's side
```

Short Chorus:
```
 B             F#    G#m              E
Unashamed and unafraid I will choose to wear Your name
B         F#     G#m          E  B/D# C#m  C#m/B  F#
In a world so full of hate I will always live Your  way
```

Verse 2:
Could it be that You should put on human flesh?
Your glory laid aside, bruised for me
Majesty upon the cross, forsaken and despised
When I think of what it cost for You
To bring me to the Father's side

Long Chorus:
```
 B          F#   G#m             E
Unashamed and unafraid I will choose to wear Your name
B        F#    G#m         E
In a world so full of hate I will always live Your way
 B         F#    G#m          E
Unashamed and unafraid I will love You all my days
B            F#          G#m           E B/D# C#m   C#m/B  F#
I don't care what men may say, I'm unashamed and un - a - fraid
```

Bridge:
```
C#m      C#m/B           F#
   I know some will say it's foolishness
C#m        C#m/B            F#
   You can't make a blind man see
C#m     C#m/B             F#
   But I know that there is power in the cross
C#m   C#m/B           F#
   To  save those who believe
```

Taken from UNASHAMED (live)
Paul Oakley
SURCD070

AND AFTER ALL

Unashamed

Paul Oakley

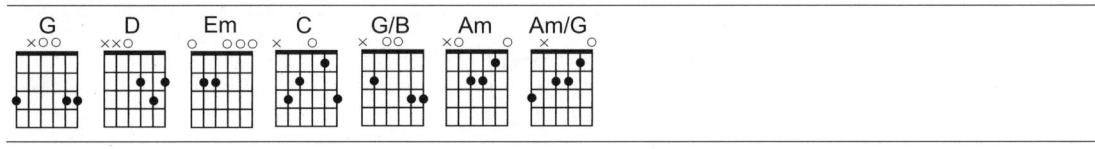

(Capo 4)

Verse 1:
```
G              Em        C            G
  And after all,    everything I once held dear
           D          Em   C
Just proved to be so vain
G              Em              C            G
  To lose it all     and find a friend who's always near
           D          Em   C
Could only be my gain
D                                        C   G
  And when I think of what You've done for me
Em           C              D
   To bring me to the Father's side
```

Short Chorus:
```
G              D      Em              C
Unashamed and unafraid I will choose to wear Your name
G              D      Em          C  G/B Am  Am/G  D
In a world so full of hate I will always live Your way
```

Verse 2:
Could it be that You should put on human flesh?
Your glory laid aside, bruised for me
Majesty upon the cross, forsaken and despised
When I think of what it cost for You
To bring me to the Father's side

Long Chorus:
```
G              D      Em              C
Unashamed and unafraid I will choose to wear Your name
G              D      Em          C
In a world so full of hate I will always live Your way
G              D      Em          C
Unashamed and unafraid I will love You all my days
G              D           Em          C  G/B   Am  Am/G  D
I don't care what men may say, I'm unashamed and un - a - fraid
```

Bridge:
```
Am      Am/G            D
   I know some will say it's foolishness
Am        Am/G          D
   You can't make a blind man see
Am      Am/G            D
   But I know that there is power in the cross
Am   Am/G          D
   To  save those who believe
```

Taken from UNASHAMED (live)
Paul Oakley
SURCD070

AND I'M MADLY IN LOVE

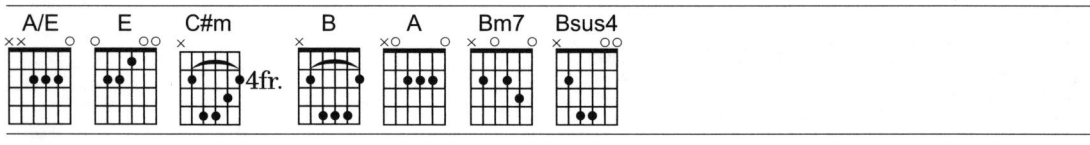

Madly

Steve Fee

A/E   E   C#m   B   A   Bm7   Bsus4

(Capo 2)

Chorus 1:
```
      A/E           E      A/E              E
And I'm madly in love with You, and I'm madly in love with You
      A/E           E      A/E              E
And I'm madly in love with You, and I'm madly in love with You
```

Section 1:
```
      C#m  B        A        E
Let what we do in here, fill the streets out there
      A      E      B      E
Let us dance for You, let us dance for You
      C#m  B        A        E
Let what we do in here, fill the streets out there
      A      E      B      E   (A E Bm7 E  x2 - 2nd time)
Let us dance for You, let us dance for You
```

Section 2:
```
      A              E
All of my life  and nothing less
      B              E
I offer to You  my righteousness
      A              E
All of my life  and nothing less
      B              E
I offer to You  my righteousness
```

Chorus 2:
```
      A           E    Bsus4           E
And I'm madly in love with You, and I'm madly in love with You
      A           E    Bsus4           E
And I'm madly in love with You, and I'm madly in love with You
```

Taken from
PASSION: OUR LOVE IS LOUD
Charlie Hall
SPD51923

Angels Gather

Paul Oakley

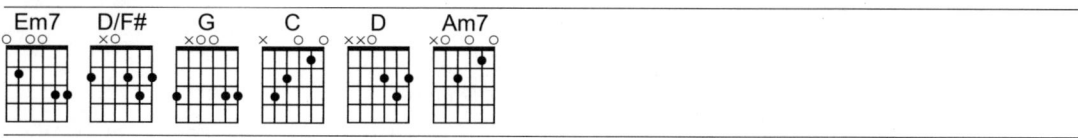

Em7   D/F#   G   C   D   Am7

Verse 1:
```
Em7        D/F#            G
   Angels gather to Your throne
            C            G
Living creatures join their song
          D        C
Singing 'holy is the Lord'
Em7        D/F#        G
   Elders tremble as they bow
           C           G
Casting down their golden crowns
          D      Em7
Crying 'holy is the Lord'
```

Chorus:
```
G                  D
  Holy are You Lord  God
Em7              C
    You are majesty,  full of mystery
G          D
  Beautiful and wise
Em7             C                    D
    You are holiness,  You are nothing less than God
   Am7  D   C
Almighty,   all glorious
```

Verse 2:
```
Worthy, worthy is the Lamb
Seated now at God's right hand
Who for sinners once was slain
Now from every tribe and tongue
Countless multitudes will come
Giving glory thanks and praise
```

Tag:
```
    Em7   D/F#    G    C
All glorious,    all glorious    (repeat)
```

Bridge:
```
D                  C
  There is no one like You,  O God
D                       C
  Every knee shall bow and every tongue confess    (repeat)
```

Taken from
BE LIFTED UP
Paul Oakley
SURCD085

James Gregory

(no capo)

Intro: C G/B Am7 F

Verse 1:
```
C                G/B                    Am7
As angels looked on You humbled Yourself
Am/G                  F
Gave up Your glorious throne
C              G/B                    Am7
Obedient to God You came to the earth
Am/G                  F
Full of compassion for us
Dm7      Am7              G
What can I do before such love
F        G    Am7
To Your majesty I bow
```

Chorus:
```
              F     C    F
You are the Almighty One
C/E          Am7 G/B C      G
You will be adored  in all the earth
C/E              F    C    F
No one is as wonderful
Dm7            G  Am7  G/B      (or to intro 1st time)
Wonderful as You
```

Verse 2:
Your great sacrifice, You gave up Your life
Such was Your passion for us
But God raised You up and now heaven sings
In praise of Your glorious cross
What can I do before such power
To Your majesty I bow

Bridge:
```
F          C   F         Am7  G
We bow down, we bow down
F       Am7              G
We bow down before You Lord      (rpt)
```

Taken from IS IT ANY WONDER
Heat
SURCD071

James Gregory

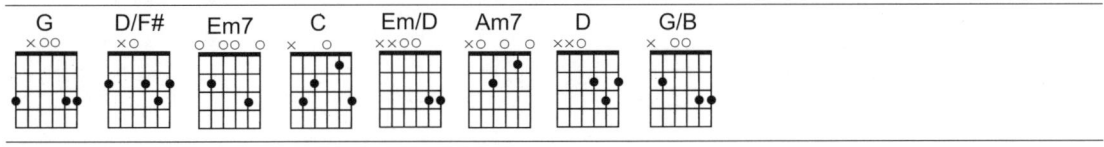

(Capo 5)

Intro: G D/F# Em7 C

Verse 1:
```
G                D/F#                Em7
As angels looked on You humbled Yourself
Em/D                 C
Gave up Your glorious throne
G            D/F#                   Em7
Obedient to God You came to the earth
Em/D              C
Full of compassion for us
Am7       Em7               D
What can I do before such love
C         D    Em7
To Your majesty I bow
```

Chorus:
```
                C     G    C
You are the Almighty One
G/B          Em7 D/F# G       D
You will be adored  in   all the earth
G/B              C    G    C
No one is as wonderful
  Am7           D   Em7  D/F#    (or to intro 1st time)
Wonderful as You
```

Verse 2:
Your great sacrifice, You gave up Your life
Such was Your passion for us
But God raised You up and now heaven sings
In praise of Your glorious cross
What can I do before such power
To Your majesty I bow

Bridge:
```
C         G  C         Em7  D
We bow down, we bow down
C         Em7           D
We bow down before You Lord     (rpt)
```

Taken from IS IT ANY WONDER
Heat
SURCD071

AS DAVID DANCED

Breathe On Me

Johnny Parks

C	G/B	Am7	F	G

Intro: C   G/B   Am7   F   x2

Verse 1:
```
          C                       G/B
As David danced, I've danced for You
          Am7                       F
I've sung the songs You've heard them too
               C              G/B
I touched the fire held in Your hands
          Am7              F
Carried my cross around this land
               C         G/B
I've held the flag, seen it fly
          Am7            F
I've prophesied into the night
               C                  G/B
I've drunk my cup and come back for more
          Am7               F
Dropped all I had to hold the sword
```

Pre-Chorus:
```
        F      G      C
And I won't give up on You
        F      G      F
And I won't give up on You
```

Chorus:
```
        C              G/B           Am7          F
Breathe on me, breathe on me, breathe on me once more      (rpt)
```

Verse 2:
And I've had doubts I'm scared to share
I've felt alone like no one's there
I have a pain that I can't shake
I have a thirst that just won't break
I need the truth deep down inside
'Cause I have dreams that I won't hide
I know this place and it isn't new
My heart still burns, still burns for You

Taken from CLOSE TO YOU
Johnny Parks
SURCD055

AS I GAZE UPON THE CROSS

Into The Arms Of Grace

Paul Oakley & Charlie Hall

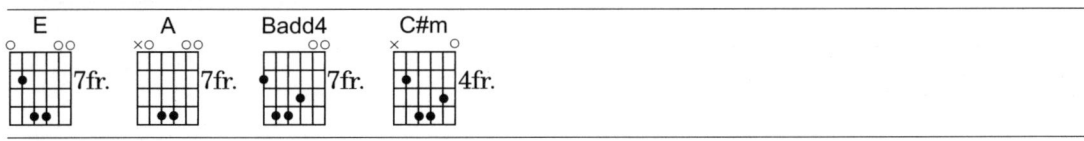

Verse 1:

E
  As I gaze upon the cross
E
  And all my sinless Saviour bore
A2   E
  I will worship, I will bow down and adore
E
  Nothing I could ever do
E
  Could ever make You love me more
A2   E
  I surrender to the wonder of it all

Chorus:

       A2   Badd4   E
And I reign in life through Your gift of grace
          A2   Badd4   E
Now Your righteousness is my own
          A2   Badd4   A2 Badd4   C#m
And the price is paid now You've made a way to come home
                      E
Into the arms of grace I run

Verse 2:

When I cease from all my striving
You turn my water into wine
I remember You alone can bring this change in me

Now for freedom I'm set free
Free to love my Saviour more
I will live for the glory of Your name

Bridge:

A2
  Never was a love so strong
E
  Never was a love so true
A2
  Giving up Your only Son
Badd4   E
       To release me from the debt I owed to You

Taken from
BE LIFTED UP
Paul Oakley
SURCD085

Trè Sheppard

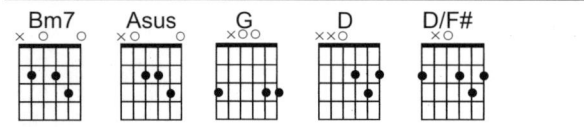

Bm7   Asus   G   D   D/F#

Intro: Bm7   Asus   Bm7   G   x2

Verse 1:
```
        D          D/F#         G
At the foot of the cross where I kneel in adoration
D    D/F#              G
And I lay my burdens down
        D          D/F#         G
I exchange all my sin for the promise of salvation
D          D/F#         G
And Your name across my brow
```

Verse 2:
At the foot of the cross I give up my vain ambition
And I leave my selfish pride
In the peace that is there would You restore my vision
In all the places I am blind

Chorus:
```
Bm7    Asus           G
  I will wait here at the cross      We will wait here at the cross
Bm7    Asus           G
  I will wait here at the cross      We will wait here at the cross
Bm7    Asus           G
  I will wait here at the cross      We will wait here at the cross
Bm7    Asus           G
  I will wait here at the cross      We will wait here at the cross
```

Verse 3:
At the foot of the cross there is healing for this nation
There is rest for those who wait
And the love that we find is the hope of all creation
We are stunned by what You gave

Verse 4:
We will wait at the cross a hungry generation
With our broken hearts and lives
Will You hear? Will You come? Will You fill our desperation?
Oh God let this be the time

Taken from CARDIPHONIA
100 Hours
SURCD073

BE LIFTED UP

Paul Oakley

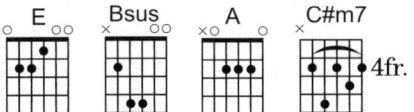

Chorus:
```
          E
Be lifted up
          Bsus
Be lifted up
          A         Bsus
As we bow down
              E
Be lifted up        (Repeat)
```

Verse:
```
A                   E
  Let the heavens rejoice
                    A
Let the nations be glad
                         E
Let the whole earth tremble
                A
For You are God
                      C#m7
Come and worship the Lord
                    Bsus
In the beauty of holiness
```

Tag:
```
          A         Bsus
As we bow down
              E
Be lifted up
          A         Bsus
As we bow down
              E
Be lifted up
```

Taken from UNASHAMED (live)
Paul Oakley
SURCD070

BEEN SEARCHING ALL MY LIFETIME

Someone I Can Live For

Ken Riley

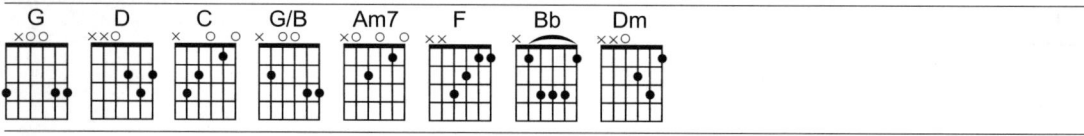

Verse 1:
G   D
  Been searching all my lifetime
G   D
  Been reaching for a lifeline
G   D
  Now I have You living inside
C   G/B   Am7
  I take a ride on the wings You give me
G   F F/G F
  And fly into Your arms

Chorus:
D   C
You are someone I can live for
F   G
You are someone I can die for
D   C   [F   G [First Chorus]
You are someone I can live for [You.]
[Second Chorus]
Bb C
You…

Verse 2:
Every day I die to survive
Strip away my self and my pride
Searching for the new man inside
I take a dive in the depths You give me
And fall into Your arms

Instrumental Bridge:
A F D C
A F D C

Taken from
REVOLUTION
YFriday
SURCD093

BEFRIENDED

Matt Redman

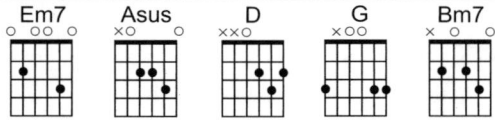

Verse 1:
```
   Em7       Asus                        D
Befriended, befriended by the King above all kings
   Em7       Asus                        D
Surrendered, surrendered to the friend above all friends
```

Verse 2:
```
  Em7    Asus                 D
Invited, invited deep into this mystery
   Em7       Asus              D
Delighted, delighted by the wonders I have seen
```

Chorus:
```
                G    Em7    Asus
This will be my story
                 D
This will be my song
                   G Em7  Asus
You'll always be my Saviour,   Jesus
                   D
You will always have my heart
```

Verse 3:
```
   Em7       Asus                         D
Astounded, astounded that Your gospel beckoned me
   Em7        Asus                  D
Surrounded, surrounded but I've never been so free
```

Verse 4:
```
  Bm7        Asus                      D
Determined, determined now to live this life for You
          Bm7        Asus                      D
You're so worthy my greatest gift would be the least You're due
```

With low E tuned to D, chords are…

```
   G          Em7        Asus
 000x        0000        00xx
        5fr.         7fr.
```

Taken from
WHERE ANGELS FEAR TO TREAD
Matt Redman
SURCD074

BLESSED BE YOUR NAME

Matt & Beth Redman

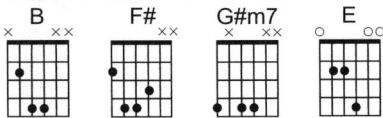

(no capo)

Verse 1:
B   F#   G#m7   E
Blessed be Your name in the land that is plentiful
               B   F#   E
Where Your streams of abundance flow, blessed be Your name
B   F#   G#m7   E
Blessed be Your name when I'm found in the desert place
              B   F#   E
Though I walk through the wilderness, blessed be Your name

Pre-Chorus:
B   F#   G#m7   E
Every blessing You pour out I'll turn back to praise
B   F#   G#m7   E
When the darkness closes in Lord still I will say

Chorus:
              B   F#
Blessed be the name of the Lord
           G#m7   E
Blessed be Your name
              B   F#
Blessed be the name of the Lord
           G#m7 F# E
Blessed be Your glorious name

Verse 2:
Blessed be Your name when the sun's shining down on me
When the world's 'all as it should be', blessed be Your name
Blessed be Your name on the road marked with suffering
Though there's pain in the offering, blessed be Your name

Bridge:
   B   F#   G#m7   E
You give and take away, You give and take away
     B   F#   G#m7   E
My heart will choose to say Lord blessed be Your name

Taken from
WHERE ANGELS FEAR TO TREAD
Matt Redman
SURCD074

Matt & Beth Redman

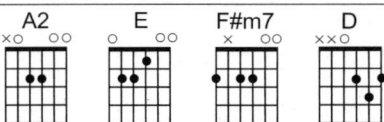

A2 E F#m7 D

Capo 2

Verse 1:
A2   E   F#m7   D
Blessed be Your name in the land that is plentiful
             A2   E   D
Where Your streams of abundance flow, blessed be Your name
A2   E   F#m7   D
Blessed be Your name when I'm found in the desert place
             A2   E   D
Though I walk through the wilderness, blessed be Your name

Pre-Chorus:
A2   E   F#m7   D
Every blessing You pour out I'll turn back to praise
A2   E   F#m7   D
When the darkness closes in Lord still I will say

Chorus:
              A2   E
Blessed be the name of the Lord
            F#m7   D
Blessed be Your name
              A2   E
Blessed be the name of the Lord
            F#m7 E   D
Blessed be Your glorious name

Verse 2:
Blessed be Your name when the sun's shining down on me
When the world's 'all as it should be', blessed be Your name
Blessed be Your name on the road marked with suffering
Though there's pain in the offering, blessed be Your name

Bridge:
     A2   E   F#m7   D
You give and take away, You give and take away
     A2   E   F#m7   D
My heart will choose to say Lord blessed be Your name

BREAK OUR HEARTS

Beyond Us

Johnny Parks

G	Em7	A7sus4	C2	D

Verse 1:

```
G  Em7         A7sus4
     Break our hearts Lord
G  Em7               A7sus4
     With what breaks Yours
G  Em7       A7sus4
     Help us use our hands
G  Em7      A7sus4
     In this broken world
```

Pre-Chorus:

```
C2      A7sus4
```

Chorus:

```
         G               D
More than seeing, more than thinking
          Em7           C2
More than praying, more than talking
         G               D
More than doing, more than giving
          Em7           C2
More than working, more than living
```

Verse 2:

```
You love all people Lord
You love this world
So will You help us Lord
To love like You do
```

Tag:

```
          G             D
We need You Lord, we need You Lord
        Em7
You are good, You are just, will You move beyond us
             C2
We need You Lord     (repeat)
```

Taken from
ON THE STREETS
Festival Manchester 2003
SURCD095

BREATHE YOUR BREATH IN ME

Lift

Ken Riley

A   D   Bm7   E   Dsus4   F#m7   Bsus4

Verse 1:
```
A                        D2       D
  Breathe Your breath in me so I can sing
A                        D2       D
  Breathe Your life that changes everything
         Bm7                    E              A Dsus4   D
Though I won't forget the way I was before You took me in
A                  D2       D
  Set a raging fire beneath my skin
A                    D2     D
  Fan the flames and purify again
       Bm7                          E
For I walk along the way You set before my feet
         Bm7                          E
As the shadows try to charm me from the light
```

Chorus:
```
            A        D2   D
Lord I lift You high tonight
                A        D2   D
Further than my dreams can fly
           Bm7              E
Way beyond the stars floating in the sky
         A        Dsus4  D
I lift You high
```

Verse 2:
Hope is where the heart of wisdom seeks
Faith is sure of what she cannot see
As I kneel before You now You tell me rise again
For my burden is much lighter in Your hands

Bridge:
```
F#m7                      D
Higher than the heavens, more than I can know
B                    E
All my heart is singing, I'll never let You go
```

Chorus 2:
Lord I lift You high tonight
Further than my dreams can fly
Way beyond the stars floating in the sky
Way beyond my heart will compromise
I lift You high...   (repeat line as necessary)

Taken from
REVOLUTION
YFriday
SURCD093

Glorious God

James Gregory

(no capo)

Intro: Bb   F   Gm7   F   x2

Verse 1:
Bb   F   Gm7   Eb
By Your power You made the earth
Bb   F   Gm7   Eb
You fashioned people by Your greatness
Bb   F   Gm7   Eb
Spoke the light that fills the lands
Bb   F   Gm7
Shining Your light in the darkness
Eb   F   Eb/G
You will shine throughout eternity

Chorus:
Bb   D7
You will be praised forever
Eb   F   D7
Your fame will know no end
Gm7   F/A   Bb   Eb   F
The nations sing together what a glorious God
Bb   F   Bb
What a glorious God

Verse 2:
In Your mercy You saw us
Though our hearts were still divided
Took our shame and gave us life
Shining Your light in our darkness
You will shine throughout eternity

Bridge:
D7   Gm7   Gm/F   Eb   Bb   F   D7
And You will be the One shining like the glorious Son
          Gm7   Gm/F   Eb   Bb   F   D7
And all around Your throne all creation will bow down
             Gm7   Fsus   F
To You the mighty King of all

Taken from IS IT ANY WONDER
Heat
SURCD071

BY YOUR POWER
Glorious God

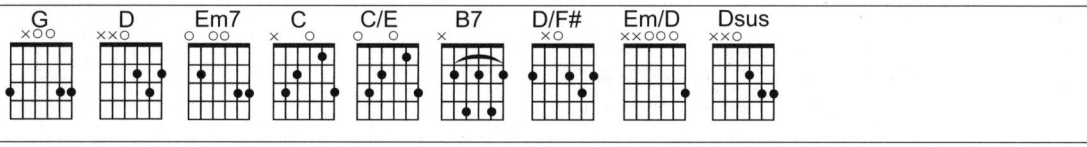

(Capo 3)

Intro: G   D   Em7   D   x2

Verse 1:
```
G                    D              Em7    C
By Your power You made the earth
G                    D              Em7    C
You fashioned people by Your greatness
G                    D              Em7    C
Spoke the light that fills the lands
G                    D              Em7
Shining Your light in the darkness
C           D                 C/E
You will shine throughout eternity
```


Chorus:
```
G             B7
You will be praised forever
C                 D        B7
Your fame will know no end
Em7         D/F#              G    C     D
The nations sing together what a glorious God
G        D        G
What a glorious God
```


Verse 2:
In Your mercy You saw us
Though our hearts were still divided
Took our shame and gave us life
Shining Your light in our darkness
You will shine throughout eternity

Bridge:
```
B7           Em7     Em/D  C              G     D    B7
And You will be the One shining like the glorious Son
          Em7        Em/D  C              G     D    B7
And all around Your throne all creation will bow down
            Em7           Dsus      D
To You the mighty King of all
```

Taken from IS IT ANY WONDER
Heat
SURCD071

Matt Redman

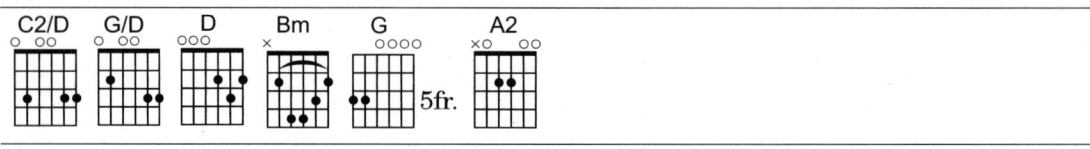

C2/D   G/D   D   Bm   G   A2

(Low E string tuned down to D)

Verse 1:
       C2/D   G/B   D   C2/D   G/B   D
Can we walk upon the water if our eyes are fixed on You?
        C2/D   G/B   D   C2/D   G/B   D
There's an air of faith within us for a time of breaking through
       C2/D G/B   D   C2/D   G/B   D
Can we fly a little higher, can we soar on eagles wings?
         C2/D   G/B   D   C2/D G/B   D
Come and fan the flames of fire that are flicker - ing within

Verse 2:
Can we walk into the promise of abundance in the land?
Take us on beyond the river to the harvest You have planned
Let us see Your Kingdom coming in a measure we've not seen
There has been a time of sowing, could this be a time to reap?

Chorus:
Bm   D   G
   Lead us to the promised land, all that's purposed, all that's planned
                   D
Give us eyes of faith again
Bm   D   G
   Take us on to higher ground and the greater things to come
               A2   C2   D
Where the eagles soar   and where we're finding more of You

Tag:
   C2   D   C2   D
And can we sing the songs of heaven while we're standing on the earth?
C   D   C2   D
 Sing within the coming Kingdom, sing and live and breathe and move
      C2   G/B   D   C2 G/B   D
Can we fly a little higher, can we fly a little higher?   (rpt)

Taken from FRIENDSHIP & THE FEAR
Matt Redman
SURCD001

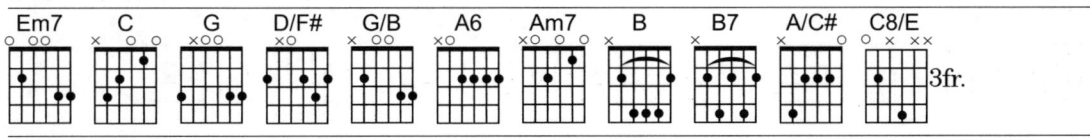

Intro: Em C G D/F# x2

Verse 1:

Em   C
Caught up in the world today I search for my escape where
      G   D/F#
I feel loved, I feel loved
Em   C
Written in my heart I find Your Word exploding through me
        G   D/F#
Like a flood, the deepest flood
      C   G/B   A6   Am7
I've spoken as angels but I need one thing

Chorus:

Em   D/F# G   C   B   B7
Love,   I'm surrounded by Your love
Em7 D/F# G   C   B   B7
Love,   I surrender to Your love

Verse 2:
Walking on the higher way of certain sacrifice
You saved us all, saved us all
As I follow let me find a passion God to love
My neighbour more, so much more
My faith's moved the mountains but I need one thing

Bridge:

C   G/B
  Love is patient, love is kind,   not a monster with green eyes
A/C#   C8/E
    Doesn't boast and it isn't proud   or raise itself way above the crowd
C   G/B
  It is for hope and it is for good,   turns its cheek when misunderstood
A/C#   C
    Always trusts, always saves, and hopes you'll run the race

Taken from
REVOLUTION
YFriday
SURCD093

CREATOR GOD

Each Day

James Gregory

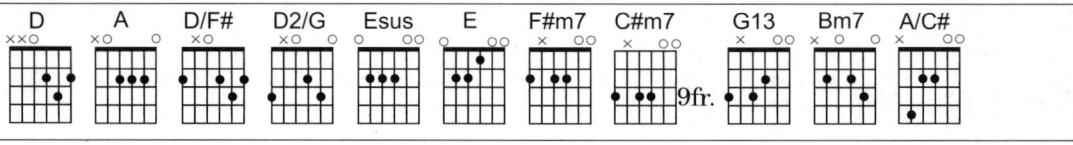

D A D/F# D2/G Esus E F#m7 C#m7 G13 Bm7 A/C#

Intro: D   A   D   A

Verse 1:
```
D        A D            A
Creator God, You made all things
D            A D/F#        A
You showed yourself in works of power
D        A D      A
Placed in our hearts eternity
D            A D/F# A
You breathed Your life into us all
D/F#       D2/G          Esus    E
Opened our eyes to seek for You
```


Chorus:
```
A           F#m7                C#m7
Each day may I find Your grace in my life
            D      E
For I am made in Your image
A           F#m7                C#m7
So help me to see Your beauty in me
                 D         C#m7   E
That touches the world around me
```


Link:
```
F#m7  G13  A  A   F#m7  G13  A  E
F#m7  G13  A  A   F#m7  G13  A  E
```


Bridge:
```
          Bm7  A/C#  E
Help me touch the world
          Bm7  A     E
Help me touch the world
          Bm7  A/C#  E
Help me touch the world
          Bm7  A     E
Help me touch the world
```

Taken from IS IT ANY WONDER
Heat
SURCD071

DAY AFTER DAY

Tim Hughes

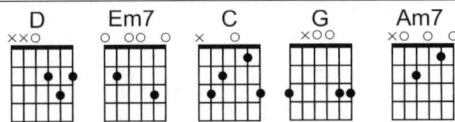

(Capo 2)

Intro: E (D) F#m7 (Em7) D (C)   E (D) F#m7 (Em7) D (C)

Verse 1:
E (D)   F#m7(Em7)
Day after day
     D (C)
I'll search to find You
E (D)   F#m7 (Em7)
Day after day
     D (C)
I'll wait for You
        E (D)   F#m7 (Em7)
The deeper I go
        D (C)   E (D) F#m7 (Em7)   D (C)
The more I love Your name

Chorus:
                    A (G) E (D)   Bm7 (Am7)
So keep my heart pure and my ways true
     A (G) E (D)   D (C)
As I fol - low   You
              A (G)   E (D)   Bm7 (Am7)
Keep me hum - ble, I'll stay mindful
           A (G)   E (D)   D (C)
Of Your merc - ies   Lord

Verse 2:
I'll cherish Your Word
I'll seek Your presence
I'll chase after You with all I have
For one day I know I'll see You face to face

Taken from HERE I AM TO WORSHIP
Tim Hughes
SURCD053

Gareth Robinson

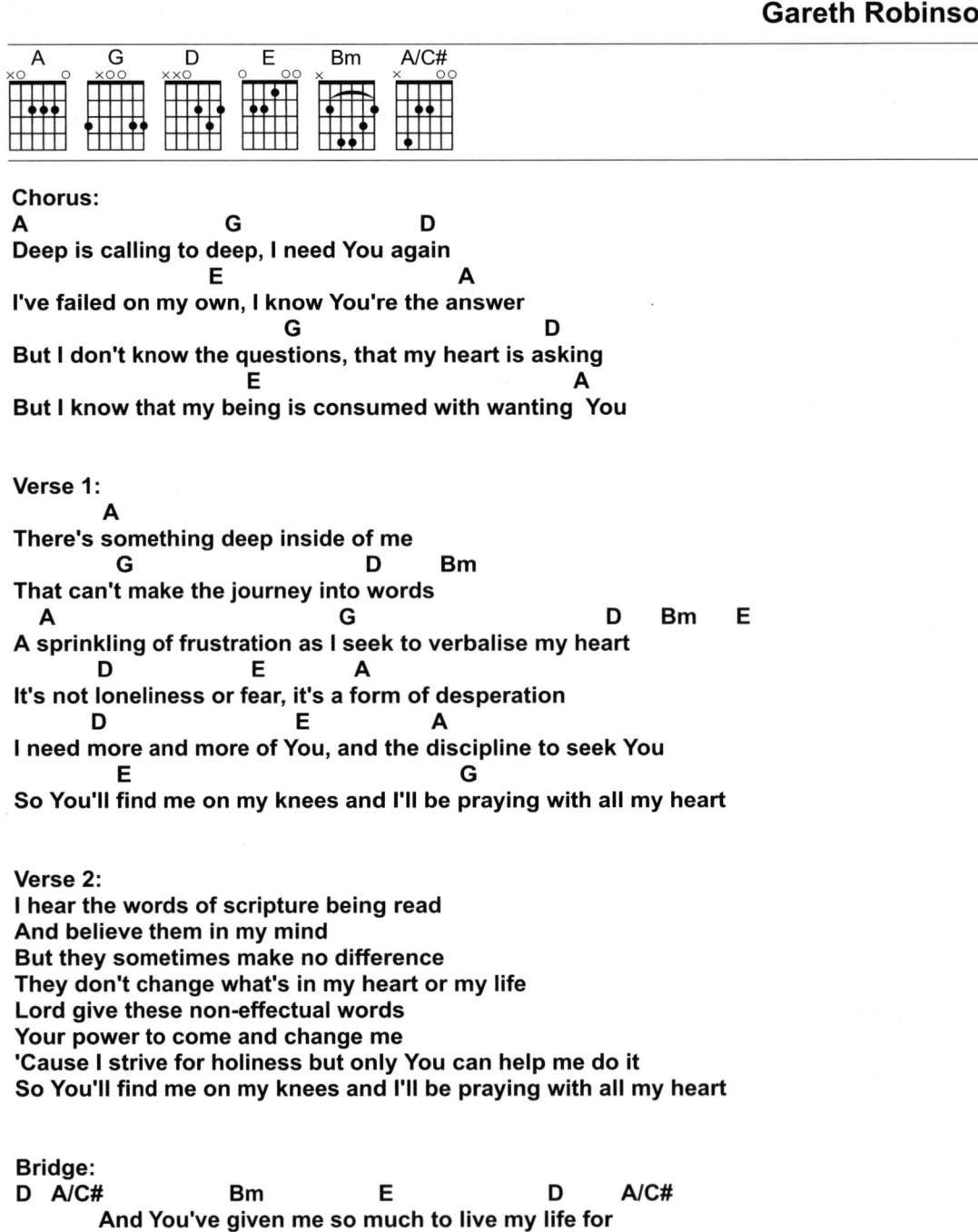

Chorus:
A   G   D
Deep is calling to deep, I need You again
                  E   A
I've failed on my own, I know You're the answer
                     G   D
But I don't know the questions, that my heart is asking
                  E   A
But I know that my being is consumed with wanting You

Verse 1:
       A
There's something deep inside of me
       G   D   Bm
That can't make the journey into words
  A   G   D   Bm   E
A sprinkling of frustration as I seek to verbalise my heart
     D   E   A
It's not loneliness or fear, it's a form of desperation
     D   E   A
I need more and more of You, and the discipline to seek You
      E   G
So You'll find me on my knees and I'll be praying with all my heart

Verse 2:
I hear the words of scripture being read
And believe them in my mind
But they sometimes make no difference
They don't change what's in my heart or my life
Lord give these non-effectual words
Your power to come and change me
'Cause I strive for holiness but only You can help me do it
So You'll find me on my knees and I'll be praying with all my heart

Bridge:
D A/C#   Bm   E   D   A/C#
       And You've given me so much to live my life for
     Bm   E   D   A/C#
You've come into my heart and made me whole
    Bm   E   D   G
So I die unto myself and live for Jesus alone

Taken from
YOU ALONE
Gareth Robinson
KMCD2494

Extravagant Worship

Vicky Beeching

Bm7	D2/G	D2	A7sus4	Em7	D2/F#	C2

Capo 2

Intro: Bm7   D2/G   D2   A7sus4   Bm7   D2/G   D2   A7sus4   x2

Verse 1:
Bm7   D2/G   D2   A7sus4
Doesn't matter what people say
Bm7   D2/G   D2   A7sus4
I   forget their watching eyes
Bm7   D2/G   D2   A7sus4
I just   want to bring to You
Em7   D2/F#
My most costly, my most precious
D2/G   Em7   A7sus4
My most priceless sac - rifice

Chorus:
  D2/G   D2/F#   A7sus4   Bm7
Extra   -   vagant wor   -   ship
D2/G   D2/F#   A7sus4   Bm7
To   -   tal surren   -   der
D2/G   D2/F#   A7sus4   Bm7
Reck   -   less aban   -   don
Em7   D2/F#   A7sus4
I pour out my love, pour out myself
    Bm7   D2/G   D2   A7sus4   Bm7   D2/G   D2   A7sus4
Saviour

Verse 2:
Bm7   D2/G   D2   A7sus4
Breaking open   my thankful heart
Bm7   D2/G   D2   A7sus4
I   re - lease its praise perfume
Bm7   D2/G   D2   A7sus4
Here I'll linger, lifting to You
Em7   D2/F#
Songs of wonder, songs of worship
D2/G   C2   A7sus4
Songs of deepest gratitude

Instrumental Bridge:
Bm7   D2/F#   D2/G   D2/G
Bm7   D2/F#   D2/G   D2/G
Bm7   D2/F#   D2/G   D2/G
Bm7   D2/F#   D2/G   D2/G

Taken from SHELTER
Vicky Beeching
SURCD083

Extravagant Worship   **Vicky Beeching**

Intro: C#m7 A E Bsus4   C#m7 A E Bsus4   x2

Verse 1:
C#m7   A   E   Bsus4
Doesn't matter what people say
C#m7 A   E   Bsus4
I   forget their watching eyes
C#m7 A   E   Bsus4
I just want to bring to You
F#m7   E/G#
My most costly, my most precious
A   F#m7 Bsus4
My most priceless sac - rifice

Chorus:
   A E/G#   Bsus4 C#m7
Extra - vagant wor - ship
A E/G#   Bsus4 C#m7
To - tal surren - der
A   E/G#   Bsus4 C#m7
Reck - less aban - don
F#m7   E/G#   Bsus4
I pour out my love, pour out myself
     C#m7 A E Bsus4   C#m7 A E Bsus4
Saviour

Verse 2:
C#m7   A   E   Bsus4
Breaking open my thankful heart
C#m7 A   E   Bsus4
I re - lease its praise perfume
C#m7 A   E   Bsus4
Here I'll linger, lifting to You
F#m7   E/G#
Songs of wonder, songs of worship
A   D Bsus4
Songs of deepest gratitude

Instrumental Bridge:
C#m7 E/G# A A
C#m7 E/G# A A
C#m7 E/G# A A
C#m7 E/G# A A

Taken from SHELTER
Vicky Beeching
SURCD083

DRAW ME CLOSE

All I Want

James Gregory

Chord diagrams: D, G/B, D/F#, Asus, G, Em7, Bm, Bm/A, D/A

Intro: D G/B D/F# Asus

Verse 1:
D   G/B
Draw me close
D/F#   Asus
Hold me near
D   G/B
Take my arms
D/F#   Asus
Carry me

Pre-Chorus:
   D/F# G   D/F# G
All I want, all I am
        G   Asus
All I ever want to be
   D/F# G   D/F# G
My resolve, my desire
         G   Asus
Is to worship You

Chorus:
            D   D/F#
I come and bow
G   Em7   D/F# G
Before my King
            D   D/F#
I come and bow
G   Em7   D/F# G
Before my King
         Bm Bm/A   Em7
Lay down my all,   my everything
G   D/A G/B   D/A   Asus
Now make me live   in You again

Tag:
D   G/B   D/F#   G
Hallelujah,   Hallelujah
D   G/B   D/F#   G
Hallelujah,   Hallelujah

Taken from IS IT ANY WONDER
Heat
SURCD071

DRAW ME NEAR

Dave Doran

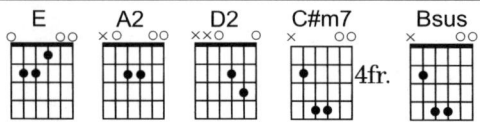

E   A2   D2   C#m7   Bsus

Verse 1:
```
E               D2
Draw me near to You
E               D2
Can I come so close
   C#m7    Bsus      A2
That I can hear Your song of love
      C#m7      Bsus      A2
That heals my broken heart
```

Chorus:
```
                   E               A2
And I will walk with You another footstep now
                   E               A2
Can we walk on again another footstep now
               C#m7                        A2
I've walked in fields of pain, I've sheltered in Your love
                     C#m7              A2
In the valley of death's shadow, I will fear no evil
                  C#m7      A2
For You are here with me
             D2            E
My comfort be, my comfort be
```

Verse 2:
Draw me near to You
Even closer still
So I can see Your scars of love
That saved my wounded soul

Taken from the
INTERNATIONAL PEOPLE'S ALBUM
Soul Survivor
SURCD054

EVEN WHEN WE TURNED

Thank You For The Cross

Brenton Brown

Intro: Am7   G/B   D   D   x3
Am7   G/B   C2   C2

Verse 1:
```
          C2          D     Em7
Even when we turned our backs on You
              C2       D        Em7
In wickedness and lies suppressed Your truth
              C2          D    Em7
Even then You showed Your love for us
         C2    D        G
Giving up Your life upon the cross
```

Chorus:
```
      Am7      G/B      D
Jesus thank You for the cross
       Am7      G/B      D
For the blood that sets us free
           Am7   G/B     D
The crimson stain of all our sin
        Am7   G/B     C2
Washed away in Your mercy
```

Verse 2:
Enemies of God with no excuse
Knowing what was right we turned from You
Given up to sin condemned to die
Even then You chose to give us life

Bridge:
```
D2/C#      C2           G/B     C2
     Everyone of us deserves to die
D2/C#            C2           G/B       C2
     But You save all who hope in Your great love
```

Taken from HOLY
Vineyard Music UK
VMUKCD06

EVERLASTING GOD

Yesterday Today and Forever

Vicky Beeching

D/F# G Bm7 A Em7
(chord diagrams)

Capo 3

Intro: D/F# G Bm7 A x2

Verse 1:
G　　　　　Bm7
Everlasting God
　　　G　　　　　　Bm7
The years go by but You're unchanging
G　　　　　Bm7
In this fragile world
　　　G　　　　　　Bm7
You are the only firm foundation

Pre-Chorus:
Em7　　　　　　　　　D/F#
　　Always loving always true
G　　　　　　　　　Bm7　　　A
　Always merciful and good, so good

Chorus:
D/F#　G　Bm7　　　A
Yesterday, today and forever
D/F#　　　　G　Bm7　　　　A
You are the same, You never change
D/F#　G　Bm7　　　A
Yesterday, today and forever
Em7　　　　　　　　G　　A
You are faithful and we will trust in You

Verse 2:
Uncreated One
You have no end and no beginning
Earthly powers fade
But there is no end to Your kingdom

Bridge:
G　　　D/F#
Yahweh, God unchanging
G　　　D/F#
Yahweh, firm foundation　　(repeat)

Taken from SHELTER
Vicky Beeching
SURCD083

EVERLASTING GOD

Yesterday Today and Forever

Intro: F/A   Bb   Dm7   C   x2

Verse 1:
Bb   Dm7
Everlasting God
     Bb   Dm7
The years go by but You're unchanging
Bb   Dm7
In this fragile world
        Bb   Dm7
You are the only firm foundation

Pre-Chorus:
Gm7   F/A
     Always loving always true
Bb   Dm7   C
   Always merciful and good, so good

Chorus:
F/A   Bb   Dm7   C
Yesterday, today and forever
F/A   Bb   Dm7   C
You are the same, You never change
F/A   Bb   Dm7   C
Yesterday, today and forever
Gm7   Bb   C
You are faithful and we will trust in You

Verse 2:
Uncreated One
You have no end and no beginning
Earthly powers fade
But there is no end to Your kingdom

Bridge:
Bb   F/A
Yahweh, God unchanging
Bb   F/A
Yahweh, firm foundation   (repeat)

Taken from SHELTER
Vicky Beeching
SURCD083

EVERYDAY
The Eyes Of My Heart

Matt Redman

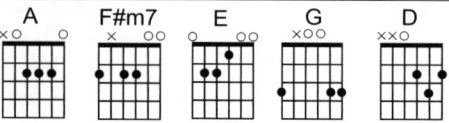

(Capo 3)

Verse 1:
C (A)   Am7 (F#m7)   G (Esus)
Everyday I see more of Your beauty
C (A)   Am7 (F#m7)   G (E)   Bb (G)
Everyday I know more of my frailty,   Lord
              F (D)   C (A)
And I can only hope that I'll be changed
Bb (G)   F (D)   G (E)
Even as I look upon Your face

Chorus:
          C (A)   Am7 (F#m7)
For the eyes of my heart
       Bb (G)
They are on You forever
       F (D)
They are on You forever
         C (A)   Am7 (F#m7)
Yes, the eyes of my heart
       Bb (G)
They are on You forever
       F (D)
They are on You forever

Verse 2:
Everyday I see more of Your greatness
Everyday I know more of my weakness
And I can only hope that I'll be changed
Even as I look upon Your face

Bridge:
C (A)
Jesus, I'm in love with You
 Am7 (F#m7)
Jesus, I'm in love with You
 Bb (G)   F (D)
Jesus, I'm in love with You Lord

Taken from HERE I AM TO WORSHIP
Tim Hughes
SURCD053

EVERY DAY I TRY AND TRY

Happy On My Way

Paul Oakley

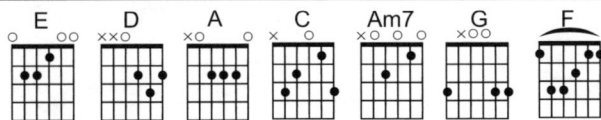

Intro: E D : A   x2
Verse 1:
E
 Every day I try and try
                              D
I really want to live my life to You
A   E
 Only to You
E
 I'm coming closer every day
                              D
I'm happy on the narrow way with You
A   E
 Only with You

Chorus:
              D   A   E
But I want to be more like You
              D   A   E
See You in me more, shine through
              D   A   E
I want to share me with You
        D   A   E
And I find my life is hidden in Your love

Verse 2:
I know my weaknesses too well
Your love is more than I can tell
But the enemy comes to kill and to destroy
I know Your work in me is strong
I'm putting all the armour on
But I know sometimes I fail to stand my ground
Chorus 2:
But You only see me like You
And only You in me shines through
You only see me win through
And I find my life is hidden in Your love

Bridge:
C   Am7   G   D
 And when I realize You've given me Your righteousness
                       A
There's no more striving
C   Am7
 You'll never change Your mind, You were for me all the time
       F   D
You take my breath away, You're more than I can say

Taken from UNASHAMED (live)
and WHEN DEEP CALLS TO DEEP
Paul Oakley
SURCD070 & SUR CD007

All I Want

Paul Oakley & Martin Cooper

D   A   G   Bm   F#m7   C2   Asus

Verse 1:
D   Asus   G
  Everyday I wake to find You there
 A   D
Singing to me
      Asus   G
Every place I go I know You're there
      A   Bm
You're always with me
    F#m   G
Every time I see the summer skies
   A   C2   G   A
I search the endless blue just to see You

Chorus:
     D   Asus   G
Because I want to be in love with You
    A
Now and forever
D   Asus   G
I wanna spend my life with You
      A   Bm
Wanna stay together
           G
Now I've found the truth
     A   D   Asus   G   A
All I want is You

Verse 2:
When I close my eyes
I see You there in risen glory
And when I'm on my knees
I know You know every little thing
And when I still my heart to hear Your voice
I hear the angels sing 'Hallelujah'

Bridge:
Bm   G
  So take some time to look and see
Bm
  Sun and moon and stars
 Asus   D A G A
And all creation speaks of You

Taken from UNASHAMED (live)
Paul Oakley
SURCD070

FATHER LET ME DEDICATE

Be Glorified   Louie Giglio, Matt Redman, Jesse Reeves, Chris Tomlin & Lawrence Tuttiet (d. 1897)

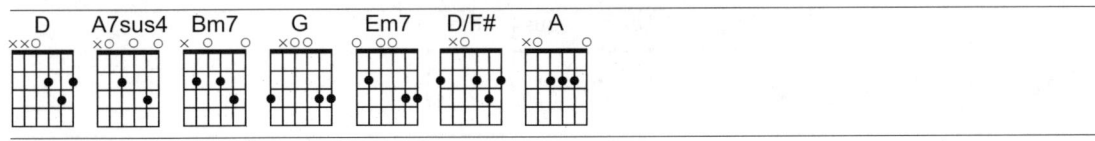

D A7sus4 Bm7 G Em7 D/F# A

(Capo 3)

Verse 1:
F (D)   C7sus4 (A7sus4)
Father let me dedicate
Dm7 (Bm7)   Bb (G)
All this life to thee
F (D)   C7sus4 (A7sus4)
In whatever worldly state
Dm7 (Bm7)   Bb (G)
Thou wilt have me be
Gm7 (Em7)   F/A (D/F#)
Not from sorrow, pain or care
Bb (G)   C (A)
Freedom dare I claim
                   Bb (G)
This alone shall be my prayer
C7sus4 (A7sus4)   F (D)
        Glorify thy name

Chorus:
F (D)   Bb (G) F (D) C (A)
  Be glorified   in   me
         Bb (G) F (D) C (A)
Be glorified
         Bb (G) F (D) C (A)
Be glorified   in   me
         Bb (G) F (D) C (A)
Be glorified

Verse 2:
Can a child presume to choose
Where or how to live?
Can a Father's love refuse
All the best to give?
Let my glad heart, while it sings
Thee in all proclaim
And, whate'er the future brings
Glorify Thy name

Verses by Lawrence Tuttiet (1825-1897)
Adpt. Matt Redman

Needing You

Vicky Beeching

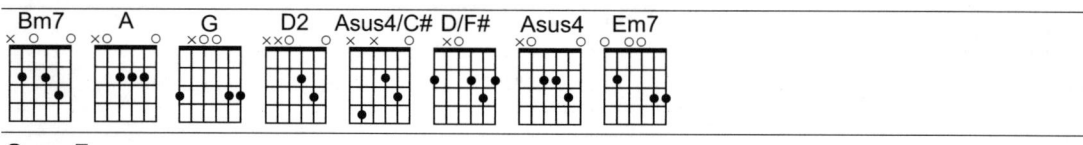

Capo 7

Intro: Bm7 A G   Bm7 A G

Verse:
D2   Asus4/C#
Father You are my shelter
              D/F#   G   Asus4
You are my place to rest and hide
D2   Asus4/C#
Father You're my creator
              D/F#   G   Asus4
You are the One who gives me life
Em7   G   Asus4
I can't live without You even for a day
Em7   D/F# G   Asus4
Laying down my pride I simply say

Chorus:
Bm7 A   Bm7 A
I am needing You
     G   D/F#   Em7 Asus4
And I'll be needing You a lifetime long
Bm7 A   Bm7 A
I am needing You
     G   D/F#   Em7
And as I offer up this fragile song
D/F# G   Asus4   Bm7 A G   Bm7 A G
In my weakness You are strong

Taken from SHELTER
Vicky Beeching
SURCD083

Needing You   **Vicky Beeching**

Intro: F#m7 E D   F#m7 E D

Verse:
A   E/G#
Father You are my shelter
            A/C#   D   E
You are my place to rest and hide
A   E/G#
Father You're my creator
            A/C#   D   E
You are the One who gives me life
Bm7   D   E
I can't live without You even for a day
Bm7   A/C# D   E
Laying down my pride I simply say

Chorus:
F#m7 E   F#m7 E
I am needing You
        D   A/C#   Bm7   E
And I'll be needing You a lifetime long
F#m7 E   F#m7 E
I am needing You
         D   A/C#   Bm7
And as I offer up this fragile song
A/C# D   E   F#m7 E D   F#m7 E D
In my weakness You are strong

Taken from SHELTER
Vicky Beeching
SURCD083

FOREVER IN MY HEART

The Promise Of The Cross

Matt Redman

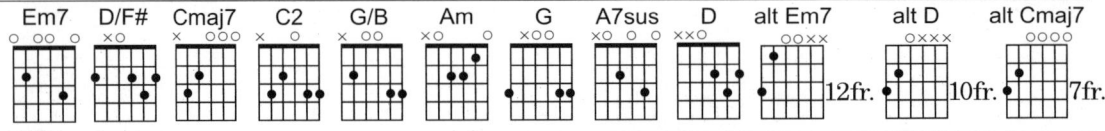

Verse 1:
Em7   D/F#   Cmaj7
Forever in my heart
               D/F#   Em7
And written on my soul
        D/F#   Cmaj7   D/F#
The promise of Your cross
Em7   D/F#   Cmaj7
I have no other claim
               D/F#   Em7
I have no other plea
        D/F#   Cmaj7   C2   G/B   Am
The promise of Your cross, the hope for every heart

Chorus:
            G   Em7
Where mercy ever flows, and shame's no longer known
 A7sus   C2   G
I praise You for the cross, the promise of Your cross to me
   G   Em7
It never fails to bring, the cleansing that I need
 A7sus   C2   G   D
I praise You for the cross, the promise of Your cross to me

Verse 2:
Embedded in my heart, and rooted in my soul
The promise of Your cross
It seals me as Your own and tells me I am Yours
The promise of Your cross, the hope for every heart

Verse 3:
Tell it in all the earth, sing it throughout the world
The promise of Your cross
There is a higher way, there is a higher hope
The promise of Your cross, the hope for every heart

Taken from
WHERE ANGELS FEAR TO TREAD
Matt Redman
SURCD074

GOD OF ALL COMFORT

Spontaneous Song

Tim Hughes

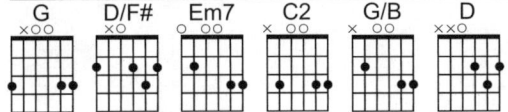

G   D/F#   Em7   C2   G/B   D

Verse:
G   D/F#
God of all comfort
Em7   D/F#
Faithful and true
G   D/F#   Em7   D/F#
Fall on Your children in Your mercy   (repeat)

Chorus:
    C2   G/B
And meet us in this place Lord
C2   Em7   D
Meet us as we wait for You
C2   G/B
Meet us in this place Lord
C2   Em7 . D   C2
Meet us as we wait for You to come

Chorus 2:
    C2   G/B
And Lord we choose to worship
    C2   Em7   D
And Lord we choose to worship You
    C2   G/B
And Lord we choose to worship
C2   Em7   D   C2
Give our all and worship only You

Taken from
GLIMPSES OF GLORY
Soul Survivor Live 2002
SURCD082

GOD OF GLORY

Glorious

James Gregory

A   Asus4   D   E   Bm7   F#m   A/C#

Verse 1:
A   Asus4   A
  God of glory and of grace
        Asus4   A
God of wisdom, God who saves
     Asus4   D   E
All creation sings the wonder of Your name
A   Asus4   A
  God of power, God who reigns
        Asus4   A
God revealed in time and space
       Asus4   D   E
And our hearts declare the wonder of Your name

Chorus:
D   A   Bm7   F#m E
  You are glorious,   You are glorious
D   A   E
  We will worship You, Our wonderful God
D   A   Bm7   F#m E   D
  You are glorious,   forever glorious(ly Lord)
        A   E
We will worship you, our wonderful God

Verse 2:
God, our refuge and our strength
God, our shield and our defence
Let the nations fear the wonder of Your name
Yours the kingdom and the power
Yours the glory forever
Let our mouths declare the wonder of Your name

Tag:
    Bm7   A/C#   D   E
Our wonderful God,   our wonderful God
    Bm7   A/C#   D   E
Our wonderful God,   our wonderful God
    Bm7   A/C#   D   E
Our wonderful God,   our wonderful God
    Bm7   A/C#   E
Our wonderful God,   our wonderful God

GOD OF HOLINESS

Glorious One

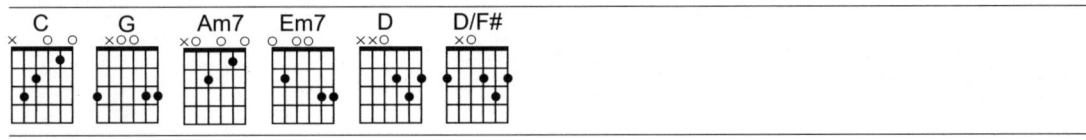

Verse 1:
```
     D (C)              A (G)
God of holiness, God of faith
     D (C)                A (G)
God of righteousness, God of grace
    Bm7 (Am7)   D (C)       F#m7 (Em7)
God of all I am,         everything
     D (C)        Bm7 (Am7)       E (D)
How I long to gaze upon Your shining face
```

Chorus:
```
       D (C)    E (D)      A (G)     F#m7 (Em7)
Beautiful Saviour,  Glorious One
          D (C)      E (D)       A (G)      F#m7 (Em7)
Awesome in splendour,  wonderful God
     D (C)        E (D)     F#m7 (Em7)        E/G# (D/F#)
My heart is overcome, my heart is overcome
     D (C)        E (D)          A (G)
My heart is overcome, glorious One
```

Verse 2:
God of purity, God of might
God of mystery, clothed in light
Through eternity we will sing
Heavens' song of love unto our glorious King

Taken from
SONGS OF HEAVEN
YFriday
YFCD02

GOD OF WONDER
I Won't Let The Rocks Cry Out

Trè Sheppard

D Em7 C2 G D/F# C/G G/B

Intro: D Em7 C2 G x2

Verse 1:
```
D        Em7            C2
God of wonder, hope and grace
              G
My heart is for You
D        Em7            C2
You fill my life with love and faith
         G
And I adore You
```

Pre-Chorus:
```
Em7  D  C2 Em7        D   C2
So I'll be singing, my heart I'm bringing     So we'll be singing, our hearts we're bringing
Em7            D      C2           D
These sounds they're ringing out for You      These sounds they're ringing out for You
```

Chorus:
```
      C2            D   G      C2    D : G
And I won't let the rocks cry out            And we won't let the rocks cry out
   C2            D   G   Em7      D   C2
I won't let the rocks cry out, my heart for You   We won't let the rocks cry out
      C2            D   G      C2    D : G
And I won't let the rocks cry out            And we won't let the rocks cry out
   C2          D   G
I won't let the rocks cry out                We won't let the rocks cry out
Em7      D  C2 Em7        D   C2
My heart for You, my heart for You           Our hearts for You, our hearts for You
```

Verse 2:
```
All the angels come and bow
And it's all for You
And we will join them with our lives
For we adore You
```

Tag:
```
   Em7        D/F#      C/G      G/B    D
Hallelujah, Hallelujah, Hallelujah, Hallelujah   (rpt)
```

Taken from CARDIPHONIA
100 Hours
SURCD073

GOD YOU ARE FULL OF GRACE

To Love The Lost

Rex Allchurch

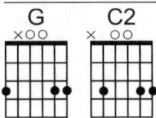

Intro: G   C2   G   C2

Verse 1:
G
God You are full of grace and mercy
        C2
And I'm standing in the light
             G   C2
Of all You've done for me
G
God You are giving me compassion
        C2
And You teach me what it is
          G
To love the lost

Chorus:
        C2
To love the lost
        G
With all my heart
        C2
Pick up my cross
        G
And follow You

Verse 2:
God please teach me how to weep as You weep
For all the broken hearted
And make me effective in my gifting
That I can see Your glory falling here

Taken from
TO LOVE THE LOST
Rex Allchurch
RACD001

GOD YOU ARE MY GOD

Glory

Johnny Parks

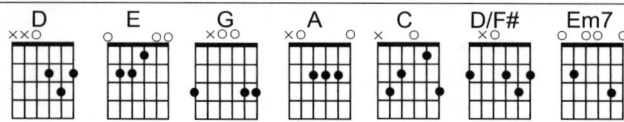

Intro: D E G A   x4

Verse 1:
```
D              E       G           A
God You are my God, there's no one else like You
     D            E   G              C : A
You gladly gave Your blood to bring me back to You
D          E   G          A
I will sing Your praise I will lift Your name
      D          E   G              A
I'll gladly give You all to see Your kingdom reign
```


Pre-Chorus:
```
    G                    D/F#
And I won't be ashamed when I lift up Your name
      Em7              A
To let all the world see that You are the king        (rpt)
```

Chorus:
```
           D E G   A
We give You glory,  glory to You
           D E G    C : A
We give You glory,  glory to You              (rpt)
```


Verse 2:
```
 D         E       G       A
Death is overcome, forgiven is my sin
  D         E        G          C : A
Heaven is my home, You've welcomed me in
   D           E      G              A
And I can't wait to hear the saints join in one song
          D         E     G         A
As we praise the loving Son who's given us His all
```

Taken from CLOSE TO YOU
Johnny Parks
SURCD055

GOOD AND GRACIOUS

Gareth Robinson

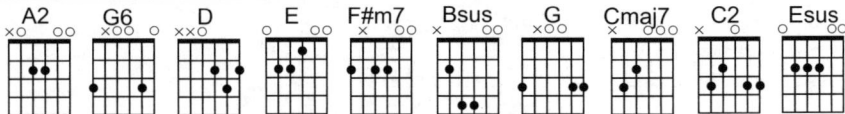

Verse 1:
```
   A2          G6          D           E
Good and gracious, attributes of a loving Father
         A2          G6         D          E
You're high and mighty but humble all the same
        F#m7              Bsus
You have made the heavens and the earth
           D           E
And You made us in Your image Lord
```

Chorus:
```
  A2    G    D          E
Holy, holy, holy is the Lord Almighty
        A2    G    D          E
And we rejoice in You alone for You are worthy
       F#m7          Bsus
And You have given life to me
       F#m7          Bsus
And I love to worship at Your feet
         D            E            A2
And I love to love You just for who You are
```

Verse 2:
```
Death and hell are now no longer things I fear
Because You have saved me and I'm grateful to the core
I'm Your child because of Jesus' blood
And Your Spirit leads me, guides me, fills me
```

Bridge:
```
  G           Cmaj7          G             C2
I'm so grateful for the things that You have given me
       G             Cmaj7             D    Esus  E
Your love, Your grace, Your joy, Your peace and more
```

Tag:
```
A2   G   F#m7  G
Ho - ly,   ho - ly   (rpt)
```

Taken from GRACE
Live Worship from New Wine 2001
KMCCD2335

GREAT IS YOUR NAME

Marc James

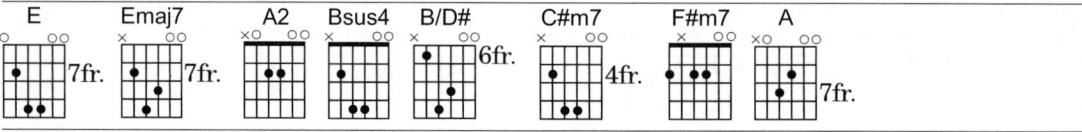

Intro: E   Emaj7   A2   Bsus4   x2

Verse 1:
E
Great is Your name
    B/D#
You suffered such pain
C#m7
So I could live
A2
Free from my shame
E
You gave Your life
B/D#
There on the cross
C#m7
Before all men
A2
You paid the cost

Pre-Chorus:
F#m7   A2
    What kind of love would do this for me?
F#m7   A2   Bsus4
    Who is this man dying for me?

Chorus:
E Emaj7   A
Praise   the Lord
E Emaj7   A
Praise   the Lord
E Emaj7   A
Praise   the Lord
E Emaj7   A
Praise   the Lord

Taken from
BEAUTIFUL
Burn : UK
VMUKCD07

HALLELUJAH
There Will Be No Other

Matt Redman

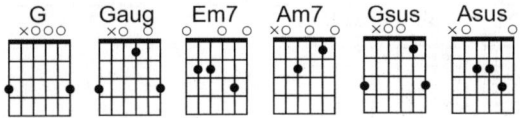

G   Gaug   Em7   Am7   Gsus   Asus

(Capo 2)

Intro: A (G)   Aaug (Gaug)   F#m7 (Em7)   Bm7 (Am7)   x2

Chorus:
   A (G)   Aaug (Gaug)
Hallelujah there will be no other
 F#m7 (Em7)   Bm7 (Am7)
Hallelujah   there will be no other
   A (G)   Aaug (Gaug)
Hallelujah there will be no other
F#m7 (Em7)   Bm7 (Am7)
There will be no other but You

Verse:
     A (G)
In the north and in the south
    Asus (Gsus)
Every corner of the globe
     F#m7 (Em7)
For the weak and for the strong
     Bm7 (Am7)
With the young and with the old
    A (G)
On and on Your praises run
     Asus (Gsus)
It's an everlasting song
F#m7 (Em7)   Bm7 (Am7)
There will be no other but You
       A (G)   Bsus (Asus)
Your song will be heard in all of the earth
       A (G)
You will have Your praise

Taken from THE FATHER'S SONG
Matt Redman
SURCD38

HAVE YOU HEARD?

Out On The Streets

Bryn Haworth

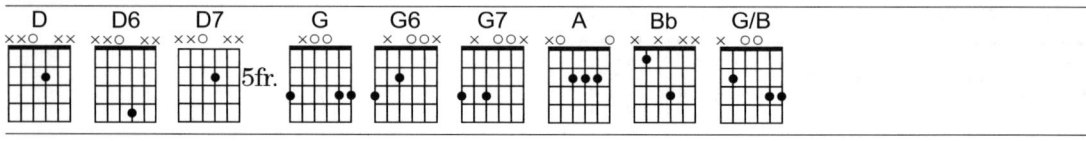

Chorus:

            G G6 G7
Have you heard?
 G G6 G7   D D6 D7   D D6 D7
The Word is out on the streets
            G G6 G7
Have you heard?
 G G6 G7   D D6 D7   D D6 D7
The Word is out on the streets
         A
We'd better get ourselves ready
 A Bb(octave) G/B   D D6 D7   D D6 D7
               To be His hands and His feet

Verse 1:

 D   D6 D7   D   D6 D7
Take the light of Jesus and shine it everywhere
 D   D6   D7   D   D6 D7
Go through towns and cities and cover them with prayer
 D   D6 D7   D   D6 D7
Sing it on street corners and in the marketplace
 D   D6 D7   D   D6 D7
Cry for God's compassion, see Jesus on each face

Verse 2:

I'm gonna go where Jesus sends me, I'm gonna forget my pride
Get out on the streets, Lord I wanna be a fool for Christ
And lift up Your name above all gods
We're gonna tell them of Your mercy Lord and tell them of His love

Verse 3:

Now we'll go there in His name, with His authority
To heal the broken hearted Lord and set the captives free
So fill me Lord with boldness to speak Your words of life
Fill me with the power to be a living sacrifice

Taken from
ON THE STREETS
Festival Manchester 2003
SURCD095

HELP ME TO BE HOLY

Rex Allchurch

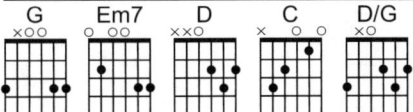

(Capo 4)

Verse 1:
B (G)
Help me to be holy

Teach me what it is

Living out this daily
G#m7 (Em7) F# (D)   E (C)
Offer   -   ing myself

Help me to be humble

Teach me what it is

Looking to You daily
G#m7 (Em7) F# (D)   E (C)
Offer   -   ing to You

Chorus:
B (G)   F#/B (D/G)   E (C)
   I long to be with You my precious
B (G)   F#/B (D/G)   E (C)
   I want to sing to You my praises
B (G)   F#/B (D/G)   G#m7 (Em7)   F# (D) E (C)   F# (D)
   I want to honour You with eve   -   ry   part of my life

Verse 2:
Guide me in my lifestyle
Teach me how to live
Follow Your example
Offering myself
Guide me in my calling
Teach me how to live
Lost in adoration
Offering to You

Taken from
TO LOVE THE LOST
Rex Allchurch
RACD001

HERE I AM

Majesty

Stuart Garrard & Martin Smith

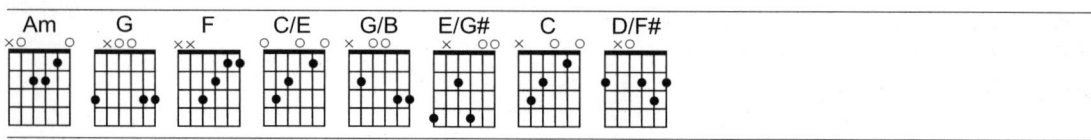

Verse 1:
Am G F   C/E   F
Here I am humbled by Your majesty
C/E   G/B   E/G#
Covered by Your grace so free
Am G F   C/E   F
Here I am, knowing I'm a sinful man
C/E   G/B   E/G#
Covered by the blood of the Lamb

Pre-Chorus:
Am G/B C   Am G/B C
Now I've found the greatest love of all   is mine
                              D/F#   F
Since You laid down Your life, the greatest sacrifice

Chorus:
C   G Am7 F
Majesty, majesty
      C   G
Your grace has found me just as I am
        Am7   F
Empty handed but alive in Your hands
C   G Am7 F
Majesty, majesty
        C   G
Forever I am changed by Your love
        Am7   F
In the presence of Your majesty

Verse 2:
Here I am humbled by the love that You give
Forgiven so that I can forgive
Here I stand knowing that I'm Your desire
Sanctified by glory and fire

HERE I BATHE

Moth To A Flame

Paul Oakley & Martin Cooper

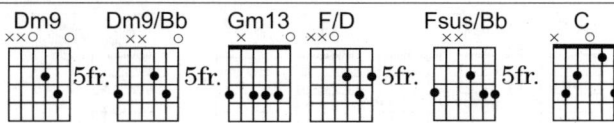

Dm9   Dm9/Bb   Gm13   F/D   Fsus/Bb   C

Intro: Dm9   Dm9/Bb   Dm9   Dm9/Bb

Verse 1:
Dm9
Here I bathe in Your light
             Dm9/Bb
I'm held by Your gaze
Dm9
Your eyes burn through my soul
           Dm9/Bb
Yet I'm not afraid
Gm13
You have seen me, known me
          Dm9/Bb
Yet I am safe
            Dm9   Dm9/Bb
Holy are You Lord

Verse 2:
Dm9
Like a moth to a flame
                Dm9/Bb
I'm drawn to Your throne
Dm9
You consume me
            Dm9/Bb
Yet I am not destroyed
Gm13
Mercy fills me, heals me
          Dm9/Bb
And I am saved

Chorus:
           F/D
Holy are You Lord
            Fsus/Bb
Far beyond words
           F/D
Holy are You Lord
            Fsus/Bb
All power and love
           C
Beauty and grace
            Fsus/Bb
Wisdom and strength
            Dm9   Dm9/Bb
Belong to You alone

Taken from UNAFRAID
Paul Oakley
SURCD081

HERE I STAND

Michael Sandeman

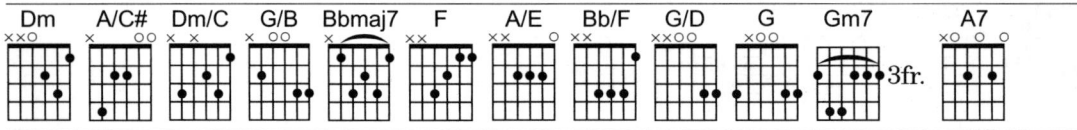

Chorus:

Dm   A/C#   Dm/C
Here I stand covered by grace
            G/B
Under the blood that was shed for me
Dm   A/C#   Bbmaj7   F
Here I kneel before the King upon His throne
Dm   A/E   Bb/F
Here I bow to worship the Lord
          G/D   Dm   F
Enjoying His favour on my life today
            Bbmaj7   G
Knowing that we'll never be apart

Verse 1:

       Dm   Gm7   Dm
I'm a child of God created for my Maker's pleasure
A7   Bbmaj7
Chosen to enjoy Him forever
       Fmaj7   A7
Granted dignity by what He says about me
Dm   Gm7   Dm
    Made in His image, precious in the eyes of my Father
A7   Bbmaj7
Purchased by the death of my Saviour
       Fmaj7   A7
I have been given life to the full

Verse 2:

In a spacious place I'm basking in the warmth of the sunshine
The Holy Spirit's tender presence
Brings such joy to me and such liberty
I'm standing firm holding fast to all He's spoken
No promise He's made will be broken
I live by faith in Jesus Christ

Bridge:

  Gm7   C/D
And I won't believe all the lies that I hear
    Gm7   C/D
When low self-esteem whispers into my ear
      Bbmaj7   Am7
That I'm worthless and poor, that I'm lost and alone
    Gm7   A7
At moments like that I must look to the throne

Taken from
NOTHING BUT THE TRUTH
Phatfish
Authentic Media

HOLY

Brenton Brown

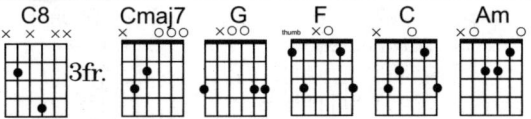

(Capo2)

Verse:
D8 (C8)
Holy Holy God Almighty
D8 (C8)   Dmaj7 (Cmaj7)
Who was and is to come
D8 (C8)
God of glory You're so worthy
D8 (C8)   Dmaj7 (Cmaj7)
All the saints bow down

Chorus:
           A (G)   G (F)   D (C)
Holy is Your name in all the earth
             A (G)   G (F)   D (C)
Righteous are Your ways so merci - ful
             A (G)   G (F)   D (C)
Everything You've done is just and true
   G (F) A (G)   D (C)
Holy Holy God are You
   G (F) A (G)   D (C)
Holy Holy God are You

Bridge:
Bm (Am)   A (G)   G (F)   D (C)
  All blessing all honour belongs to You
Bm (Am)   A (G)   D (C)
  All power all wisdom is Yours

Taken from HOLY
Vineyard Music UK
VMUKCD06

James Gregory

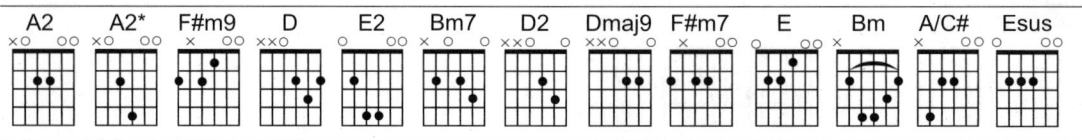

Intro: A2   A2*   F#m9   D   E2   Bm7   D2:Dmaj9   D2:Dmaj9

Verse 1:
A2   F#m7   D
How can I live without You
                    E   A2
You are the heart that beats in me
              F#m7   D
Just like the air I'm breathing
              E   F#m7
I need You deep inside of me

Pre-Chorus:
              Bm
I give my life to You
A/C#   D
How else could I live

Chorus:
A2   A2*   F#m9   D   E
I'm so glad to know You, for this reason I was made
        Bm7   D   A2
I will live to serve You, all within me will bring You praise
          A2*   F#m9   D   E
I'm devoted to You, I surrender all I am
        Bm7   D   A   F#m7   D   Esus
Be exalted greatly, reign as King and Lord of my life

Verse 2:
How can I live without You
You gave up everything for me
Forgiving my rebellion
Taking my shame away from me

Instrumental:
A7sus : A7   A7sus : A7   Bm7   G   x4

Chords for
Instrumental
Section...

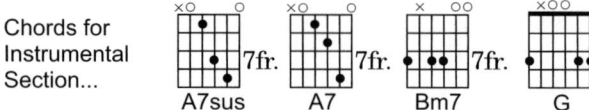

A7sus   A7   Bm7   G

Taken from IS IT ANY WONDER
Heat
SURCD071

HOW SWEET MY SAVIOUR'S NAME 62

Paul Oakley

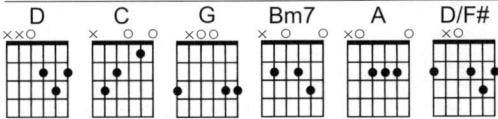

D C G Bm7 A D/F#

(Capo 4)

Verse 1:
F# (D)
   How sweet my Saviour's name
               E (C) B (G) F# (D)
It sounds like music in my ears
F# (D)
   Awake my soul and sing
                E (C) B (G) F# (D)
Come seek His presence and draw near

Verse 2:
My bread of heaven come down
My food, my drink, my every need
My pearl, my treasure found
My joy, my righteousness, my peace

Chorus:
        E (C) B (G) F# (D)
I worship You   all my days
        E (C) B (G) F# (D)
I worship You   name above all other names

Verse 3:
My prophet, priest, and king
My boast, my hope, my victory
My sacrifice, my lamb
My song through all eternity

Bridge:
D#m7 (Bm7)   E (C)   F# (D)
   Your love and faithfulness surround me
D#m7 (Bm7)   E (C)   B (G)
   Your blood has sealed me in this covenant of grace

Chorus 2 (after bridge):
        B (G) C# (A) D#m7 (Bm7)
I worship You   all my days
        B (G) C# (A) F#/A# (D/F#)
I worship You   name above all other names

Taken from
BE LIFTED UP
Paul Oakley
SURCD085

Johnny Parks

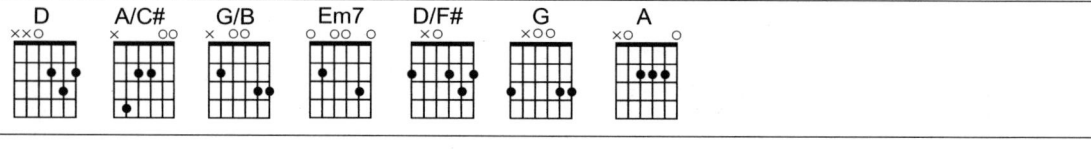

(Capo 2)

Chorus 1:
```
   E (D)                B/D# (A/C#)
I call on You Almighty Lord
  A/C# (G/B)           B/D# (A/C#)
I call on You Almighty Lord      (rpt)
```

Verse 1:
```
   E (D)                          B/D# (A/C#)
I come to You and stand before Your throne
  A/C# (G/B)                   B/D# (A/C#)
I lift my voice in worship here once more
     E (D)                       B/D# (A/C#)
You turned the darkness in me into light
    A/C# (G/B)                      B/D# (A/C#)
You took my blinded soul and gave me sight
     E (D)                          B/D# (A/C#)
As I sank down to the depths You heard my cry
    A/C# (G/B)                    B/D# (A/C#)
You lifted me and taught me how to fly
     E (D)                          B/D# (A/C#)
You promised me you're always here to stay
      A/C# (G/B)                    B/D# (A/C#)
So as I stand before You Lord I want to say
```

Chorus 2:
```
   E (D)                B/D# (A/C#)
I worship You Almighty God
  A/C# (G/B)            B/D# (A/C#)
I worship You Almighty God            (rpt)
```

Verse 2:
```
The heavenly host are captured by the love
Of the One who laid His life down at the cross
We lift the name of Jesus to the skies
So all might see and know that there is life
And where there's hatred let me bring Your love
And where there's sorrow let me bring Your joy
As I stand before You will You lift Your face
And bring resurrection power to this place
```

Instrumental Tag:
```
F#m7 (Em7)  E/G# (D/F#)  A (G)  E/G# (D/F#)
F#m7 (Em7)  E/G# (D/F#)  A (G)  B (A)
```

Taken from CLOSE TO YOU
Johnny Parks
SURCD055

I CAN ONLY IMAGINE

Bart Millard

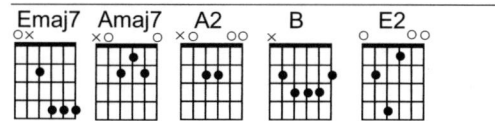

Verse 1:

   Emaj7
I can only imagine what it will be like
    Amaj7
When I walk by Your side.
    Emaj7
I can only imagine what my eyes will see
     Amaj7
When Your face is before me:
    Emaj7 Amaj7
I can only imagine.

Chorus:

 A2   B
Surrounded by Your glory, what will my heart feel?
    E2
Will I dance for You, Jesus, or in awe of You, be still?
Emaj7 A2   B
Will I stand in Your presence, or to my knees will I fall?
   E2
Will I sing 'hallelujah' - will I be able to speak at all?
  Emaj7 A2   B   Amaj7
I can only   imagine, I can only imagine. [1st time only]
  Emaj7 A2   B   E
I can only   imagine, I can only imagine. [2nd time only]

Verse 2:

   Emaj7
I can only imagine when that day comes,
   Amaj7
And I find   myself standing in the Son.
    Emaj7
I can only imagine, when all I will do,
     Amaj7
Is forever, forever worship You:
    Emaj7 Amaj7
I can only imagine

In The Waiting

Matt Redman & Todd Proctor

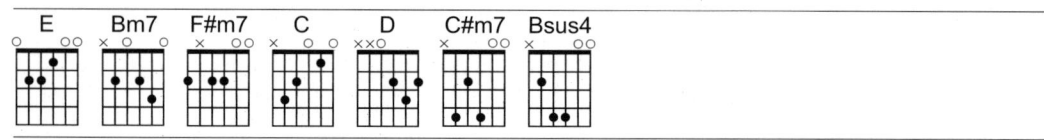

E   Bm7   F#m7   C   D   C#m7 Bsus4

Verse 1:
```
E           Bm7
  I cultivate     a quiet place
F#m7                    C  D
      Within this life of mine
E              Bm7
  I come to wait      before the One
F#m7                        C  D
      Who knows my hearts desire
           C
In the stillness I have come
     D              E
To wait before You God
```

Chorus:
```
       F#m7          C#m7   Bsus4
And I find You in the wai  -  ting
       F#m7          C#m7   Bsus4
And I find You in the wai  -  ting
       F#m7          C#m7
You remind me in the stillness
    Bsus4         C    D    E
To know You are God
```

Verse 2:
You heard my cry so long before
I ever spoke a word
You knew my name so long before
The heavens touched the earth
In the stillness I have come
To wait before You God

Taken from
**INTIMACY/
FRIENDSHIP & THE FEAR**
Matt Redman
SURCD092

I DREAM

Believer

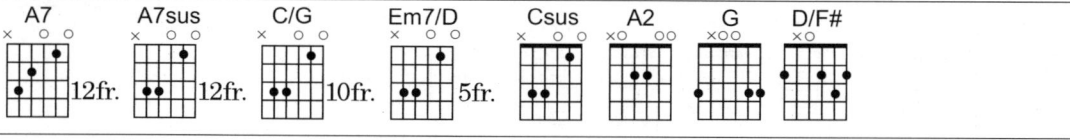

Verse 1:
A7   A7sus
  I dream of tongues of fire resting on Your people
C/G   Em7/D   Csus Em7/D
   I dream of all the miracles to come
A7   A7sus
  I hope to see the coming healing of the nations
C/G   Em7/D   Csus Em7/D
   I long to see the prodigals return

Pre-Chorus:
       Em7/D   Csus
So many hopes and longings in You
               Em7/D
When will all the dreams come true?

Chorus:
A2   G
  I'm a believer in Your kingdom
D/F#   A2
  I am a seeker of the new things
A2   G
  I am a dreamer with some old dreams
D/F#   A2
  Let them now come   (rpt)

Verse 2:
I hope to see You come down, rend the mighty heavens
And let Your glory cover all the earth
To see Your sons and daughters come to know and love You
And find a purer passion in the church

Verse 3:
May Your church now reach out sowing truth and justice
Learn to love the poor and help the weak
When Your Kingdom's coming it will touch the broken
Place the lonely in a family

Taken from THE FRIENDSHIP & THE FEAR
Matt Redman
SURCD001

Falling Down

D	D/F#	G	Em7	A	F#	F#/E	Am	Asus4

Verse 1:

      D   D/F#
I fall down on my knees
          G   Em7
To my Saviour, Almighty
  D   A   G   D
I cry, Lord I cry revival
           D   D/F#
I reach out for Your hand
          G   Em7
For Your Spirit upon our land
  D   A   G   D
I cry, Lord I cry revival

Chorus:

         D/F# G   A
I'm falling down on my knees
     D/F#   G   A
Crying out "O hear my plea"
         F#   F#/E   Am
Won't You let Your kingdom come
          G   Em7   Asus4   A
Won't You let Your will be done
        D/F#   G   A
Father God we long to see
         D/F#   G   A
Broken hearts revived and healed
     F# F#/E   Am
Jesus roll away the stone
          G   Em7 Asus4   A
Lead our generation home

Taken from
SONGS OF HEAVEN
YFriday
YFCD02

I GIVE MYSELF TO YOU

Every Last Part

Scott Anderson

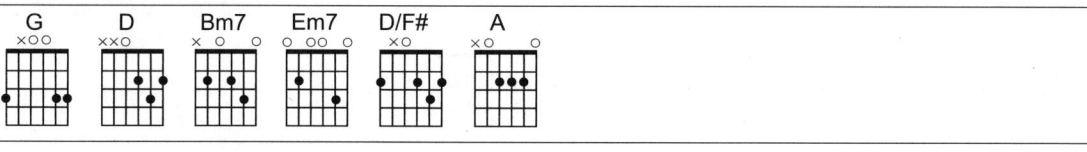

G D Bm7 Em7 D/F# A

(Capo 3)

Intro: Bb (G)   F (D)   Bb (G)   F (D)   x2

Verse 1:
F (D)   Dm7 (Bm7)
You have made the world
                            Bb (G)
You have calmed the sea
                            Gm7 (Em7)
You can move a mountain
        Bb (G)   F (D)
And You can move me
    Gm7 (Em7)   F/A (D/F#)
You have healed the sick
        Bb (G)   Gm7 (Em7)
You have raised the dead
 F/A (D/F#)   Bb (G)
Come bring Your fire
        C (A) Bb (G)
In my life again

Chorus:
Bb (G)   F (D)
I give myself to You
Bb (G)   F (D)
As I learn what You can do
Bb (G)   Dm7 (Bm7)
You can transform my heart
                    Bb (G)
Redeem every last part
                    Bb (G)
I give myself to You

Taken from the
INTERNATIONAL PEOPLE'S ALBUM
Soul Survivor
SURCD054

Gareth Robinson

Cmaj7   F   Dm7   Dm/C   G/B   G   C/E   Fmaj7

Verse 1:
Cmaj7   F
I have no one in heaven but You
     Cmaj7   F
I want nothing on earth besides You
   Dm7 Dm/C   G/B
For You alone are holy
    Dm7 Dm/C   G/B
Lord You alone are holy

Verse 2:
I have no one in heaven but You
I want nothing on earth besides You
For You alone are holy
For You alone are trustworthy

Chorus:
  G   C   C/E
So I will sing my praise to You
              F   G
For You are good, You are true
              C   C/E
No earthly thing compares to You
        F   G   C
Always faithful, ever loving mighty God

Bridge:
     Fmaj7 Cmaj7   Fmaj7   Cmaj7
And no one gives me life like You do
Fmaj7 Cmaj7   Fmaj7   Cmaj7
No one gives me peace like You do
Fmaj7 Cmaj7   Fmaj7   Cmaj7
No one gives me grace like You do
Fmaj7 Cmaj7   Fmaj7   G
No one gives me hope like You

Taken from
YOU ALONE
Gareth Robinson
KMCD2494

Belongs To You

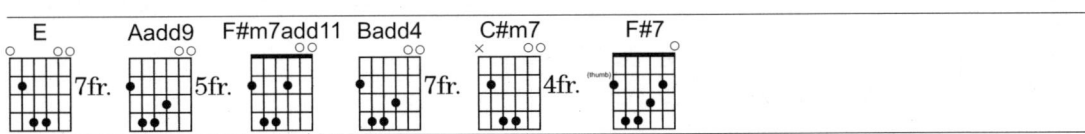

Intro: E5   Aadd9   E5   Aadd9

Verse 1:
E5   Aadd9
   I hear the tears of my Father falling
E5   Aadd9
   'Cos He's been waiting for such a long time
E5   Aadd9
   I hear the sound of His heart beat calling
E5   Aadd9
   As I discover that everything that's mine
        F#m7add11   Badd4
Belongs to Him, belongs to Him

Chorus:
       E5
Belongs to You
       Aadd9
Jesus all I have
        C#m7
Jesus all I am
       E5
Jesus all I see
       F#7
Jesus all I'll be
       Aadd9
Belongs to You

Verse 2:
I sense the chains of my resistance falling
As freedom beckons and Jesus takes me in
I feel the strain of sin but I'm no longer crawling
And repentance flows as I realise all that's within
Belongs to Him, belongs to Him

Taken from BURNOUT
Cathy Burton
FIERCD02

I JUST WANT TO LOVE

I'll Always Love You

Tim Hughes

G	D	Em7	C2	Am7	G/B
xOO	xxO	O OO O	x O	xO O O	x OO

(Capo 2)

Verse 1:
A (G)   E (D)   F#m7 (Em7)   D (C2)
I just want to love,   I just want to sing
A (G)   E (D)   F#m7 (Em7)   D (C2)
To the One above who has touched this thirsty soul
A (G)   E (D)   F#m7 (Em7)   D (C2)
I just want to love,   I just want to sing
A (G)   E (D)   F#m7 (Em7)   D (C2)
To the One above who has touched this thirsty soul
          Bm7 (Am7)
And now I'll never be the same

Chorus:
A (G)   E (D)
I'll always love You
F#m7 (Em7) D (C2)   A (G)
I'll always   sing to You Jesus
        E (D)
I long to worship You
  F#m7 (Em7)   D (C2)
In Spirit and in truth   (rpt)

Verse 2:
Everyday I'll come, spend my life with You
Learning of Your heart and what You're calling me to do
Everyday I'll come, spend my life with You
Learning of Your heart and what You're calling me to do
My every breath belongs to You

Bridge:
Bm7 (Am7)   A/C# (G/B)   D (C2) Bm7 (Am7)
And with this song we'll lift the name of Jesus higher
        A/C# (G/B)   D (C2)
And with a shout we'll raise up one voice   (optional repeat)

Taken from HERE I AM TO WORSHIP
Tim Hughes
SURCD053

I KNOW YOU LOVE

Bowing Down

Matt Redman

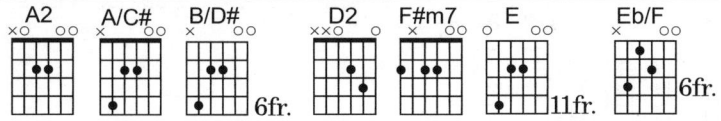

A2   A/C#   B/D#   D2   F#m7   E   Eb/F

Intro: A2   A/C#   B/D#   D2   x2

Verse 1:
```
A2          F#m7 D2            A2
I know You love   to crown the humble
   A2        F#m7 D2             A2
Pouring out grace  for the broken hearted
 A2            F#m7 D2           A2
You bless the meek, You meet the lowly
  A2      F#m7 D2        A2
Lord as I bow  lift me to You
```

Chorus:
```
  A2        A/C#       B/D#  D2
I keep on bowing down,    bowing down
  A2        A/C#       B/D#        D2
Keep on bowing down, what else can I do?
  A2        A/C#       B/D#  D2
K eep on bowing down,     bowing down
 A2            A/C#  B/D#          D2         A2  A/C#  B/D#  D2
What else can I do to give it all to You?
```

Verse 2:
I'd like to be one such believer
Keeping my knees firmly on the ground
I'd like to tread humbly before You
Lord as I bow lift me to You

Tag:
```
E       B/D#          D2                        E
 Do You smile when You see a humble believer on their knees
       B/D#          D2              Eb/F
And my Lord will You be pleased to look upon me,   to look upon me
```

Taken from FRIENDSHIP & THE FEAR
Matt Redman
SURCD001

I KNOW YOU LOVE AN OFFERING

Led To The Lost

David Gate

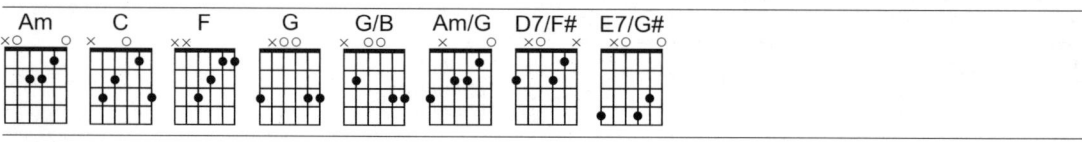

Capo 5

Verse 1:
Am
    I know You love an offering
        C   F
That's costly, outreaching
         Am   G
Touching Your heart for the poor
Am
    The songs we sing as our offering
           C   F
Are more fragrant in Your presence
    Am   G
If we live a life of love

Chorus:
C
  And as we follow Your heart
G/B
    We are led to the lost
Am   Am/G   D7/F#   G
Finding there a place of praise no matter what the cost
C
  So we will stand with the weak
G/B
    Give our most to the least
Am   Am/G   D7/F#   G
Serving You with all we have, Your kingdom God we seek
    E7/G#   Am
We are led to the lost

Verse 2:
Now I see what You command
To be faithful and humble
Putting selfish hopes aside
So change my heart that I may love
My neighbour as my brother
And to live a life of love

Taken from
ON THE STREETS
Festival Manchester 2003
SURCD095

Led To The Lost

David Gate

Verse 1:
```
Dm
    I know You love an offering
        F        Bb
That's costly, outreaching
            Dm           C
Touching Your heart for the poor
Dm
    The songs we sing as our offering
        F           Bb
Are more fragrant in Your presence
      Dm        C
If we live a life of love
```

Chorus:
```
F
  And as we follow Your heart
C/E
      We are led to the lost
Dm            Dm/C          G7/B          C
Finding there a place of praise no matter what the cost
F
  So we will stand with the weak
C/E
      Give our most to the least
Dm              Dm/C         G7/B            C
Serving You with all we have, Your kingdom God we seek
        A7/C#      Dm
We are led to the lost
```

Verse 2:
```
Now I see what You command
To be faithful and humble
Putting selfish hopes aside
So change my heart that I may love
My neighbour as my brother
And to live a life of love
```

Taken from
ON THE STREETS
Festival Manchester 2003
SURCD095

I LIVE MY LIFE

Just To Be With You

Gareth Robinson

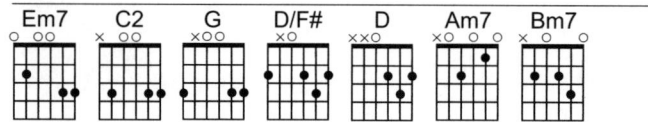

(Capo 1)

Verse 1:
       Fm7 (Em7)   Db2 (C2)
I live my life to worship You
          Fm7 (Em7)   Db2 (C2)
I spend my days serving You
      Ab (G)   Eb/G (D/F#)
Now I come
  Fm7 (Em7) Db2 (C2)
I come

Verse 2:
I want to spend some time with You
To steal away and be with You
So now I come, I come

Chorus:
      Ab (G)   Eb/G (D/F#)
Just to be with You
      Fm7 (Em7)   Db2 (C2)
Just to know more of Your love
     Ab (G)   Eb (D)
Just to be with You
      Db2 (C2)   Bbm7 (Am7)
And to love You

Bridge:
Cm7 (Bm7)   Bbm7 (Am7)
   And here You know me
Cm7 (Bm7)   Bbm7 (Am7)
   And here You love me
Cm7 (Bm7)   Bbm7 (Am7)
   And here I know You
Cm7 (Bm7)   Bbm7 (Am7)
   And here I love You

Taken from
YOU ALONE
Gareth Robinson
KMCD2494

Trust In You

Paul Oakley

(no capo)

Verse 1:
```
E          A   E              D2  A
 I love You Lord,  and I will not be   afraid
E              A       Bsus  B
  Though many enemies surround me
E          A   C#m          D2  A
 Father I know     Your loving kindness
E              A       Bsus  B
  And Your right hand sustains me
```

Chorus:
```
              E            A
You are my rock, You are my refuge
              E            A
You are my shield, You are my shelter
        F#m7                D2
You are strength, You are my song
         Bsus  B
 My everything
                E              A
You are my stronghold and my fortress
         C#m      D2  A
You're my rock, my deliverer
Bm      A             Bsus  B
  And I put my trust in You
```

Verse 2:
```
E          A   E              D2      A
 I know Your love,  I know Your faithfulness
E          D2     A    Bsus  B
 I know the promises  You gave me
E      A  C#m          D2  A
 And so I will    rest in Your favour
E              A       D2 A  Bsus  B
  Knowing Your power is within  me
```

Last line of chorus 2nd time;
```
Bm      A           E
  And I put my trust in You
D  A           E
 I put my trust in You
Bm A           E
 I put my trust in You
```

I LOVE YOU LORD
Trust In You

Paul Oakley

D	G	C2	Asus	A	Bm	Em7	Am

(Capo 2)

Verse 1:
```
D           G  D            C2  G
 I love You Lord,  and I will not be   afraid
D             G          Asus  G
 Though many enemies surround me
D          G  Bm           C2  G
 Father I know    Your loving kindness
D             G        Asus  A
 And Your right hand sustains me
```

Chorus:
```
            D              G
You are my rock, You are my refuge
            D              G
You are my shield, You are my shelter
       Em7              C2
You are strength, You are my song
          Asus  A
 My everything
            D              G
You are my stronghold and my fortress
          Bm     C2  G
You're my rock, my deliverer
Am      G          Asus  A
  And I put my trust in You
```

Verse 2:
```
D           G  D            C2     G
 I know Your love,  I know Your faithfulness
D          C2  G   Asus  A
 I know the promises  You gave me
D          G  Bm          C2  G
 And so I will   rest in Your favour
D              G     C2 G  Asus  A
 Knowing Your power is within me
```

Last line of chorus 2nd time:
```
Am      G          D
  And I put my trust in You
C  G              D
  I put my trust in You
Am  G             D
  I put my trust in You
```

Taken from UNAFRAID
Paul Oakley
SURCD081

I NEED YOU

Romance Me   **Paul Oakley & Martin Cooper**

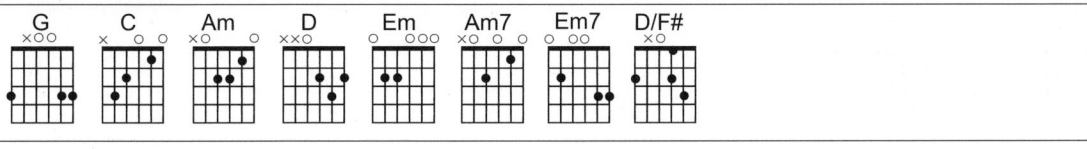

(Capo 2)

Intro: G   C   Em7   C

Verse 1:
     A (G)   D (C)   Bm (Am)   E (D)
I need You like the summer needs the sun, I need You to walk and to run
     A (G)   D (C)   Bm (Am)   E (D)
I need You like a river needs the rain, I need You to fill me again
       Bm (Am) F#m (Em)   Bm (Am)   E (D)
Without You I run dry, Without You I won't even survive

Chorus:
   A (G)
So wake me, take me with You
  D (C)
Chase me where Your river runs
  F#m7 (Em7)   D (C)
Romance me 'til my heart belongs to You
    A (G)
Oh draw me closer to You
  D (C)
Lead me in Your ways
  F#m7 (Em7)   D (C)
Enchant me because my life belongs to You

Verse 2:
I need You like the stars need the sky, I need You to help me to shine
I need You like a singer needs a song, I need You to carry on
Without You I run dry, Without You I won't even survive

Bridge:
  Bm (Am)   D (C)
Embrace me, let me feel Your strength
          F#m (Em)   E (D)
Hide me in Your shade, You're my shelter in the rain

Final chorus:
   A (G)   D (C)
So wake me, take me with You, chase me where Your river runs
  F#m7 (Em7)   D (C)
Romance me 'til my heart belongs to You
    A (G)   E/G# (D/F#)   F#m7 (Em7)   D (C)
Oh draw me closer to You, lead   me   in Your ways
   A (G)   E (D)   D (C)
Enchant me because my life belongs to You

Taken from UNAFRAID
Paul Oakley
SURCD081

I NEED YOU LIKE THE RAIN

Beautiful

Samuel Lane

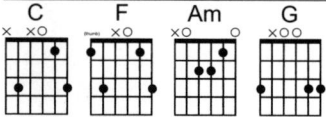

Verse 1:
C   F
  I need You like the rain
C   F
  Come to me and sing again
C   F
  I long for Your love so much
C   F
  I've wanted Your pure touch

Chorus:
Am   G   F
    You are beautiful, beautiful
               Am   G
You are beautiful, beautiful
          F   C
So beautiful, so beautiful

Verse 2:
I need You to be here
Come to me, I can feel You near
I love You, You are my hope
You love me as Your own

Taken from
BEAUTIFUL
Burn : UK
VMUKCD07

I SEE THE LORD

Paul Oakley

(no capo)

Verse 1:
```
F                          C            F
I see the Lord and He is high and lifted up
          Bb          C7sus
And His train fills the temple
F                        C           F
I see You Lord and You are high and lifted up
            Bb          C7sus
And Your train fills the temple
```

Chorus:
```
C        Bb   F  Bb          F
 And I cry ho - ly, holy is the Lord
 Bb          F    C7sus
Holy is the Lord most high
C        Bb   F  Bb          F
 And I cry ho - ly, holy is the Lord
 Bb          F    C7sus    C
Holy is the Lord most high
```

Verse 2:
I see Your holiness and light surrounds Your throne
Who am I to come before You?
But now my guilt is gone, my sins are washed away
Through Your blood I come

Bridge:
```
Bb                    C            Dm7
   Who am I that I should gain the Father's love?
Bb                     C7sus    C
   Now my eyes have seen the King
  Bb                   C            Dm7
Touch my lips that I may tell of all You've done
Gm
    Fill my heart I cry
C7sus
      Be glorified
```

Taken from DREAMS & VISIONS
Re:vive@Stoneleigh
SURCD059

I SEE THE LORD

Paul Oakley

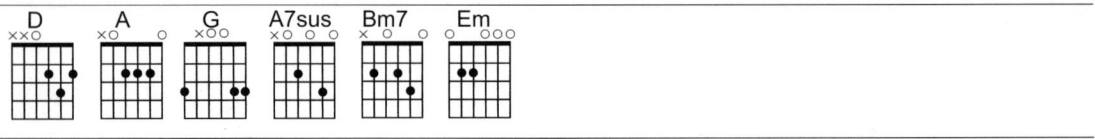

(Capo 3)

Verse 1:
```
D                         A          D
I see the Lord and He is high and lifted up
         G         A7sus
And His train fills the temple
D                        A          D
I see You Lord and You are high and lifted up
          G         A7sus
And Your train fills the temple
```

Chorus:
```
A      G  D  G        D
 And I cry ho - ly, holy is the Lord
 G         D      A7sus
Holy is the Lord most high
A      G  D  G          D
 And I cry ho - ly, holy is the Lord
  G         D      A7sus    A
Holy is the Lord most high
```

Verse 2:
```
I see Your holiness and light surrounds Your throne
Who am I to come before You?
But now my guilt is gone, my sins are washed away
Through Your blood I come
```

Bridge:
```
G                        A           Bm7
   Who am I that I should gain the Father's love?
G                        A7sus    A
   Now my eyes have seen the King
   G                A           Bm7
Touch my lips that I may tell of all You've done
Em
   Fill my heart I cry
A7sus
     Be glorified
```

Taken from DREAMS & VISIONS
Re:vive@Stoneleigh
SURCD059

Saved The Day

Ken Riley

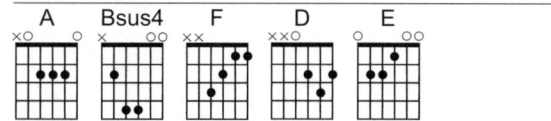

(Capo 2)

Verse 1:
  B (A)
I tried to save the world today
     C#sus4 (Bsus4)
By showing them Your face
G (F)   B (A)
With this kiss I won't give You away
     B (A)
You pick me up each time I fall
      C#sus4 (Bsus4)
And turn my life around
G (F)   B (A)
Give me strength to move to higher ground

Chorus:
               E (D)   F# (E)
Look what You've done for me
          B (A)
Look what my life can be
              E (D)
Look what You've done Lord
  F# (E)   B (A)
Your love has saved the day

Verse 2:
Why You came for one like me
I'll never understand
I have Your invitation in my hand
To dance through all eternity
With everyone who calls
Upon the name who is above them all

[End of last chorus]
           B(A)   B/A(A/G)   B/G#(A/F#)   B/F#(A/E)
Your love has saved the day.   x2
             E(D) F#(E) B(A) E(D) F#(E) B(A)
Your love has saved.... the day.

Taken from
REVOLUTION
YFriday
SURCD093

I WANT TO COME

Face To Face

Adrian Langhart

C   Am   Em   F   G

Verse 1:
C
I want to come
      Am
As close as I can
Em
To You my Lord
       F
Wherever I am

Chorus:
G   F   G   F
One day I'll see You face to face
G   F   G   F
One day I'll see You face to face
G   F   G   F
One day I'll see You face to face
          G   F
I'll see You face to face
          G   F
I'll see You face to face

Taken from the
INTERNATIONAL PEOPLE'S ALBUM
Soul Survivor
SURCD054

I WANT TO KNOW

Draw Me Nearer

Gareth Robinson

[Chord diagrams: C, F, Am, G/B, C/E, G, A, D/F#, Bm, A/C#]

Verse 1:
```
C              F              C          F
  I want to know Your pleasing and perfect will for me
  Am        G/B
So   renew my mind
C         F          C            F                Am
  Open my eyes so I can see the wonderful things You have for me
        G/B
Amazing love
```

Chorus:
```
C/E      F        C/E
Draw me nearer to You Lord
     F              Am      G/B
That I might know You more, faithful God
C/E  F        C/E
Only You can satisfy
              F              Am
Breathe on me Your breath of life          (Am into the bridge)
          G        F        G         C  F  Am  G/B
'Cause all I want to do is be a living sacrifice for You
```

Bridge:
```
Am        G    Am      G
   And if I see You,  I will know You
Am        G      Am          G
   And if I know You,   then I will love like You
Am        G    Am      G
   And if I see You,  I will know You
Am        G      Am          G                 A
   And if I know You,   then I will love like You, I  will love like You
```

Chorus 2:
```
D/F#     G           D/F#
Draw me nearer to You Lord
     G            Bm      A/C#
That I might know You more, faithful God
D/F#  G        D/F#
Only You can satisfy
              G              Bm
Breathe on me Your breath of life
              A        G         A         D  G  Bm
A/C#...
'Cause all I want to do is be a living sacrifice for You
```

Taken from
YOU ALONE
Gareth Robinson
KMCD2494

I WANT YOU TO KNOW

All I Want

Mark Underdown

D G Em7 A Bm7 D/F# Bb C

Intro: D G Em7 A x4

Verse:
D   Bm7   Em7   A
  I want You to know
D   Bm7   Em7   A
  That it's You I will follow
Bm7   A   G
    Lead me to that place
D/F#   Em7   A
    Where Your melody is made
D   Bm7 Em7 A
  Strip me apart
D   Bm7   Em7   A
  Look down deep into my heart
Bm7   A   G
    Through my brokenness
D/F# Em7   A
      Make me stronger in You

Chorus:
D   G   Em7   A
  All I want is You
D   G   Em7   A
  All I need I receive from You
D   G   Em7   A
  To be found in the truth
D   G   Em7 A D
  'Cause all I want,   all I want is You

Bridge:
Bb   C
    See the praise in the words of this song
Bb   C
    See the will, see my will to go on and on
Bb
    Still searching for You
    C   D
To take me to that place

I WAS LOST

Start Of The Summer

Ken Riley

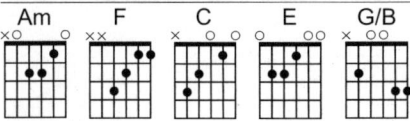

Am   F   C   E   G/B

Capo 5

Verse 1:
```
Am        F   C         E   Am
    I was lost, trapped in my own direction
 F         C          E
A bruise with no time to heal
Am   F   C         E   Am
   My life, a shadow of frail ambition
 F       C            E
A desert choking for rain
Am   F     C          E      Am
   I heard, a song drowning out my sorrow
 F        C         E
A sound of hope deep in me
Am     F   C        E   Am
   My heart, shouted the invitation
F          C          E
Come and take hold of me!
```

Chorus:
```
Am        F
Hey now, hey now
C         E         Am
I can feel the start of the summer
 F    C      E
Rising into my life
Am        F
Hey now, hey now
C         E         Am
I can feel the start of the summer
 F    C      E
Rising inside of me
```

Verse 2:
So now, I wake up and kiss the morning
The taste so sweet on my lips
I know, my spirit is joined with heaven's Son
Rising in me!

Bridge:
```
F          C          G/B
  I feel You running in my veins
              E
I hear You calling, calling me…
```

Taken from
REVOLUTION
YFriday
SURCD093

I WAS LOST

Start Of The Summer

Ken Riley

Verse 1:
Dm   Bb F   A   Dm
    I was lost, trapped in my own direction
 Bb   F   A
A bruise with no time to heal
Dm Bb F   A   Dm
   My life, a shadow of frail ambition
 Bb   F   A
A desert choking for rain
Dm Bb F   A   Dm
   I heard, a song drowning out my sorrow
 Bb   F   A
A sound of hope deep in me
Dm   Bb F   A   Dm
   My heart, shouted the invitation
Bb   F   A
Come and take hold of me!

Chorus:
Dm   Bb
Hey now, hey now
F   A   Dm
I can feel the start of the summer
 Bb F   A
Rising into my life
Dm   Bb
Hey now, hey now
F   A   Dm
I can feel the start of the summer
 Bb F   A
Rising inside of me

Verse 2:
So now, I wake up and kiss the morning
The taste so sweet on my lips
I know, my spirit is joined with heaven's Son
Rising in me!

Bridge:
Bb   F   C/E
   I feel You running in my veins
         A
I hear You calling, calling me…

Taken from
REVOLUTION
YFriday
SURCD093

I WILL LOVE YOU LORD FOREVER

Taste And See

Trè & Tori Sheppard

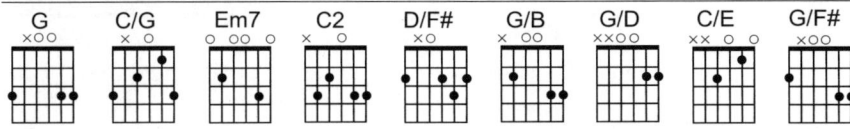

G	C/G	Em7	C2	D/F#	G/B	G/D	C/E	G/F#

Intro: G C/G G C/G   G C/G G C/G x2

Verse 1:
G   C/G   G   C/G
I will love You Lord forever
   G   C/G   G   C/G
My lips will always sing Your name
      G   C/G   G   C/G
From deep inside I feel it rising
      G   C/G   G   C/G
Come glorify the Lord with me
      G   C/G   G   C/G
Come glorify the Lord with me

Chorus:
 Em7   C2   D/F#   G
I taste and see that You are good
 Em7   C2   D/F#   G
I hide myself within Your love
Em7   C2   D/F#   G
In Your presence I lack nothing
    Em7 C2   D/F#   G   G C/G G C/G   G C/G G C/G
You're all I want and You are here with me

Verse 2:
 G   C/G   G   C/G   G C/G G C/G
I looked for You and oh You found me
   G   C/G   G   C/G   G C/G G C/G
Delivered me from all my fears
   G   C/G   G   C/G   G C/G G C/G
With hearts wide open, our faces shining
      G   C/G   G   C/G   G C/G G C/G
Our shame is gone as You draw near

Bridge:
     G   C2   G/B   C2
Come glorify the Lord with me, come glorify the Lord with me
   G/D C/E   G/F# C/G
Come glorify the Lord with me, come glorify the Lord with me
or
G   C2   G/B   C2
In Your presence I lack nothing, in Your presence I lack nothing
G/D   C/E   G/F#   C/G
In Your presence I lack nothing, in Your presence I lack nothing

Taken from CARDIPHONIA
100 Hours
SURCD073

I WILL PRAISE YOU

I Will Rejoice

Samuel Lane

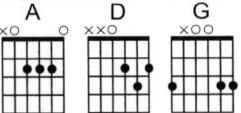

Verse 1:
A   D
  I will praise You O Lord with all my heart
A   D
  I will tell of Your wonderful deeds
A   D
  I will sing with joy because of You
A   D
  I will praise You the Almighty God

Chorus:
A   D
  I will rejoice in You
G   D
  Because You love me
A   D
  I will rejoice in You
G   D
  Because You saved me

Bridge:
G   A
  You are King forever
G   A
  You rule with righteousness
G   A
  You are my deliverer
G   A
  In You Lord I can trust

Taken from
BEAUTIFUL
Burn : UK
VMUKCD07

I WORSHIP YOU

Revolution

Ken Riley

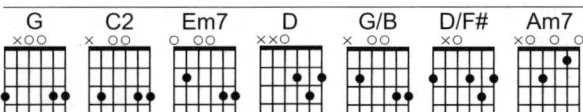

Verse 1:
```
 G      C2      G      C2
I worship You and I sing Your name
        Em7     C2          D
For my heart can dance with freedom
 G      C2      G      C2
I lift You high as a burning flame
        Em7    C2      D
As a light to all who need You
```

Pre-Chorus:
```
C2
    I'm crying for this generation
G/B
     Waiting on Your revelation
Em7                        D/F#
   I long to let Your will be done
D C2
     I'm standing in the gap and praying
G/B
     Open up the gates of heaven
Em7                        D/F#
   O God let Your kingdom come
```

Chorus:
```
      G  C2  G  C2
In revolution
    Em7  C2  D
Revolution
```

Verse 2:
```
Hear the call to the heart of man
To the world who needs a Saviour
Let the heavens shake as we make a stand
For a King who is forever
```

Bridge:
```
C2                        G/B
Change the world, come change us now
Am7              G
Change the world, invade our hearts
```

(repeat...then use last line of Pre-Chorus to get to Chorus)

Taken from
ON THE STREETS
Festival Manchester 2003
SURCD095

I'M OPEN TO YOU

Martyn Layzell

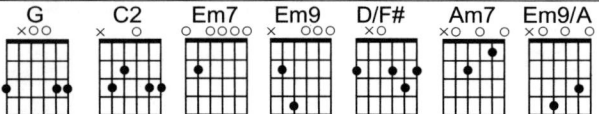

Verse 1:
```
G              C2
I'm open to You
  G            C2
So open for You
  Em7            C2
Without You I'm broken
    G          C2        G    C2
Without You I'm no one
```

Chorus:
```
G                  Em9
As I gaze into Your eyes
   C2          G   D/F#
I realise that You love me
G                   Em9
There's no need to run or hide
           C2
I come just like a child
          G  D/F#
And You love me
        Am7      Em9/A
You love me
```

Verse 2:
```
Surrendered to You
Surrounded by You
The distance between us
Is fading before us
```

Tag:
```
  Em7            C2
You love me, You love me
  Em7              C2
You love me, and I love You
  Em7            C2
You love me, You love me
  Em7              C2
You love me, and I love You
                   G  C2  G  C2
And I love You and I love You
```

Shine 2

Ken Riley

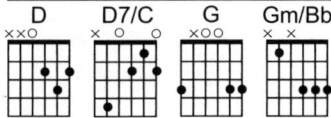

Verse 1:
```
D       D7/C                   G
  If I could, I'd wrestle with the angel
  Gm/Bb
Until You bless me
D              D7/C                  G
  I'm coming through, banging at the doorway
Gm/Bb
Let me in
```

Pre-Chorus:
```
      D                        D7/C
You know that I want You, with all of my being
G                      Gm/Bb
Searching with all the strength that's in me
      D                    D7/C
I'm seeking to find You, while You can be found
      G              Bb
But I can't wait until the morning comes so
```

Chorus 1:
```
D    D7/C         G       Gm/Bb
Shine,  shine into the darkness Lord so
D    D7/C  G   Gm/Bb
Shine    to us
```

Verse 2:
```
I've scaled the walls, and hunted through the city
For my lover
I've climbed the towers, in my desperation
To have You near
```

Chorus 2:
```
D     D7/C        G       Gm/Bb
Shine,  shine into the darkness Lord so
D    D7/C  G   Gm/Bb
Shine    to us
        D                   D7/C
As a sign in the sky, as a beacon of light
        G                   Gm/Bb
As the brightest of fires in the depths of the night so
D    D7/C  G   Gm/Bb
Shine    tonight
```

Taken from
REVOLUTION
YFriday
SURCD093

Where Angels Fear To Tread   Matt Redman & Tom Lane

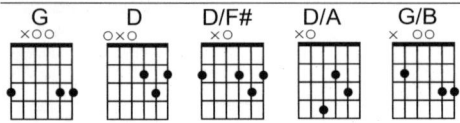

G   D   D/F#   D/A   G/B

(Capo 2 except for low E string)

Verse 1:
```
     A (G)                      E (D)
If it wasn't for Your mercy, if it wasn't for Your love
     A (G)                          E (D)
If it wasn't for Your kindness, how could I stand
     A (G)                      E (D)
If it wasn't for Your cleansing, if it wasn't for Your blood
     A (G)                      E (D)
If it wasn't for Your goodness, how could I stand
```

Pre-Chorus:
```
        E/G# (D/F#)    A (G)
And yet I find myself again
          E/B (D/A)      A/C# (G/B)
Where even angels fear to tread
          E/G# (D/F#)      A (G)
Where I would never dare to come
          E/B (D/A)        A/C# (G/B)
But for the cleansing of Your blood
```

Verse 2:
```
     A (G)                        E/G# (D/F#)
With You there is forgiveness, and therefore You are feared
     A (G)                        E/G# (D/F#)
Jesus it's Your loving kindness, that brings me to my knees
```

Chorus 2:
```
     E/G# (D/F#)          A (G)
In the beauty of Your holiness
     E/B (D/A)          A/C# (G/B)
In the beauty of Your holiness
     E/G# (D/F#)          A (G)
In the beauty of Your holiness
     E/B (D/A)          A/C# (G/B)
In the beauty of Your holiness
```

Taken from
WHERE ANGELS FEAR TO TREAD
Matt Redman
SURCD074

I'M AMAZED EVERY DAY

I'll Never Stop Loving You

Martyn Layzell

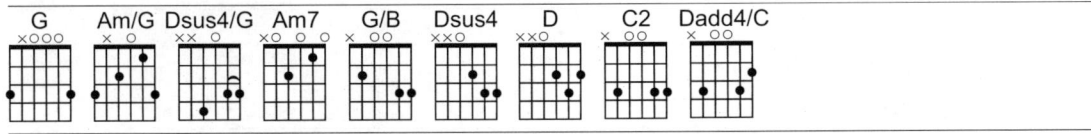

G   Am/G Dsus4/G Am7 G/B Dsus4   D   C2 Dadd4/C

Verse 1:
    G   Am/G
I'm amazed every day
         Dsus4/G   Am/G
At the newness of Your grace
      G   Am/G
Like the dawn that awakes
         Dsus4/G   Am/G
To the song of morning sun

Pre-Chorus:
Am7   G/B   Dsus4   D
Mercies new every morning
Am7 G/B   Dsus4   D
Jesus I give You glory

Chorus:
G   Am/G   C2   Dadd4/C
I'll never stop loving You
G   Am/G   C2   Dadd4/C
I'll never stop loving You
G/B   Am7   G/B   C2
All my days I'll sing Your praise
G   Am/G   C2   Dadd4/C
I'll never stop loving You

Verse 2:
Swept away by the force
Of Your Spirit's burning flame
Like a wave bound for shore
That will never cease to break

Verse 3:
You are love, You are grace
Your compassions never fade
You are joy in my pain
You're the King of endless days

Taken from
LOST IN WONDER
Martyn Layzell
SURCD076

I'M FORGIVEN

Amazing Love

Billy James Foote

E/G#   A   Bsus4   E

Verse:

E/G#   A   Bsus4
   I'm forgiven because You were forsaken
E/G#   A   E   Bsus4
   I'm accepted, You were condemned
E/G#   A   Bsus4
   I am alive and well, Your Spirit is within me
   A   Bsus4   E
Because You died and rose again

Chorus:

E   A
  Amazing love, how can it be
E   Bsus4
  That You my King would die for me
E   A
  Amazing love, I know it's true
E   Bsus4
  And it's my joy to honour You
      A Bsus4   E
In all I do I honour You

Taken from
PASSION: BETTER IS ONE DAY
Chris Tomlin
SPD0230

I'M GRATEFUL FOR THE WAY

Close To You

Johnny Parks

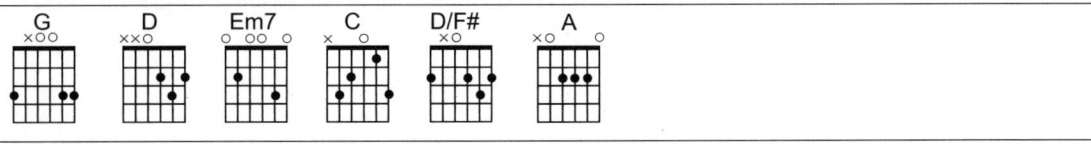

G   D   Em7   C   D/F#   A

Intro: G   D   Em7   C:D   x4

Verse 1:
```
G          D/F#        Em7       C
I'm grateful for the way You look at me
G          D/F#        Em7       C
I'm thankful that You don't give up
G                D/F#          Em7         C
You're a friend who's smiled at me a thousand times
G          D/F#             Em7         C
When I cause You pain You bring me love
```

Pre-Chorus:
```
A         C  A        C
I've found a place   where I'm free
A         C  A           C                                    D
And I'm dancing now  'cause You love me, You love me, You love me, You love me
```

Chorus:
```
G D/F# Em7  C   G   D/F#     Em7  C
 I    love You, You know it's true
G  D/F# Em7  C          G     D/F#  Em7  C
And all   I   want is to be close to You
```

Verse 2:
```
G                   D/F#            Em7       C
When I've done the worst, You've seen the best in me
G          D/F#               Em7         C
I was running away but You brought some rest to me
G          D/F#        Em7                C
My heart is Yours and I give it all to You
G          D/F#            Em7            C
And when it's tough I know You'll pull me through
```

Taken from CLOSE TO YOU
Johnny Parks
SURCD055

I'M MAKING MELODY

Making Melody

Matt Redman

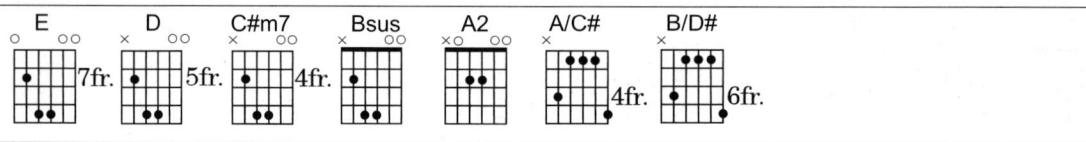

Verse 1:
E   (D)
I'm making melody in my heart to You
E
I'm making melody in my heart to You
C#m7   Bsus   A2
Pouring out Your praise
       Bsus   E
With everything within

Verse 2:
E   (D)
I'm making melody in my heart to You
E
I'm making melody in my heart to You
C#m7   Bsus   A2
Yours will always be
      Bsus   E
The song I love to sing

Chorus:
         A2   Bsus   E
How can hearts not love Your name
         A2   Bsus   E
How can souls not sing Your praise
  A2 Bsus   A/C# B/D#   E
Jesus You've put music in my soul

Taken from
WHERE ANGELS FEAR TO TREAD
Matt Redman
SURCD074

I'M WEAK BUT I'M STRONG

The Yoke Is Easy

Matt Redman

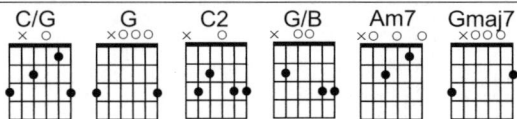

C/G   G   C2   G/B   Am7   Gmaj7

Verse 1:
```
C/G                 G
   I'm weak but I'm strong
C/G                 G
    I'm helpless but helped now
C/G               G
   I'm struggling but I
C/G            G
   Consider it joy for I know
             C/G                G
That You're with me and You're for me
          C/G                       G
And You didn't just look down from heaven above
          C/G               G
But You came down and You found me
     C/G                G            C2  G/B Am7  C2
I surrendered to mercy and gave myself up and I'm fi - na - lly   free
```

Chorus:
```
G           Gmaj7  C2          G
  And now You're with me  the yoke is easy
         Gmaj7    C2  G/B Am7  G
The load is heavy but ligh - ter   to   bear
         Gmaj7   C2          G
Now You're with me  the yoke is easy
         Gmaj7    C2 G/B Am7  G
The road is narrow but I  find  You there
```

Verse 2:
You are strength for the weak
You're the refugee's refuge
Open arms at the cross
Tell of welcome and love and of rest
For the weary and the lonely
And the hungry of heart find a place they can eat
And the journey looks costly
But to live now is Christ and to die would be gain for I'm heavenly bound

Taken from FRIENDSHIP & THE FEAR
Matt Redman
SURCD001

IS IT ANY WONDER

James Gregory

(no capo)

Intro: B   B/A   G#m7   E

Verse 1:
```
B           B/A          G#m7          E
Is it any wonder that I long to serve You
B               B/A            G#m7     E
When I think of all I'm thankful for
B           B/A          G#m7          E
Is it any wonder that my heart adores You
A                           F#
When You show Yourself so wonderful
```

Verse 2:
Is it any wonder that I love to praise You
There is so much I am thankful for
I would be a fool to ever turn away Lord
You're my Saviour and You're wonderful

Chorus:
```
B
You bring freedom You bring love
            B/A          G#m7
Grace and kindness from above
                    E  G  F#
Shining light on every situation
B
You are holy but close by
          B/A            G#m7
You're eternal but You're mine
                  E         G        F#  F#/E  B/D#  C#m
And I cannot stop my love from growing
```

Bridge:
```
   F#            F#/E              B/D#         C#m
And I'm amazed that I can know the friendship of a holy God
    F#            F#/E              B/D#      C#m
That One as powerful as You takes notice of my life
    F#              F#/E            B/D#      C#m
Keep in my mind the wonder of the incarnated God of love
F#        F#/E          B/D#           C#m
I will always live to praise You, I'm so thankful that You saved me
```

Taken from IS IT ANY WONDER
Heat
SURCD071

IS IT ANY WONDER

James Gregory

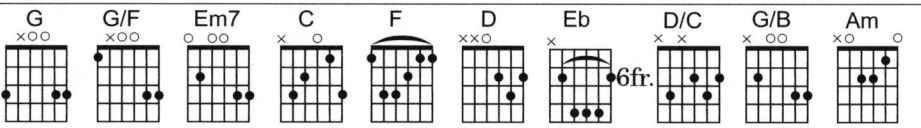

(Capo 4)

Intro: G G/F Em7 C

Verse 1:
G   G/F   Em7   C
Is it any wonder that I long to serve You
G   G/F   Em7   C
When I think of all I'm thankful for
G   G/F   Em7   C
Is it any wonder that my heart adores You
F   D
When You show Yourself so wonderful

Verse 2:
Is it any wonder that I love to praise You
There is so much I am thankful for
I would be a fool to ever turn away Lord
You're my Saviour and You're wonderful

Chorus:
G
You bring freedom You bring love
             G/F   Em7
Grace and kindness from above
                       C Eb D
Shining light on every situation
G
You are holy but close by
             G/F   Em7
You're eternal but You're mine
                C   Eb   D D/C G/B Am
And I cannot stop my love from growing

Bridge:
   D   D/C   G/B   Am
And I'm amazed that I can know the friendship of a holy God
   D   D/C   G/B   Am
That One as powerful as You takes notice of my life
   D   D/C   G/B   Am
Keep in my mind the wonder of the incarnated God of love
D   D/C   G/B   Am
I will always live to praise You, I'm so thankful that You saved me

Taken from IS IT ANY WONDER
Heat
SURCD071

I'VE BEEN CAUGHT UP

Grace

James Gregory

(no capo)

Intro: D   Esus D   Esus

Verse 1:
```
D                     Esus      D
I've been caught up with so much and
    Esus    D         Esus        D         Esus
I admit the love I had for You was growing cold
D             Esus        D
I had filled my days with things that
      Esus         D              Bm7       Esus     E
In the end don't matter, but I find You still love me
```

Chorus:
```
        A                    D         F#m7
Your grace amazes me, You love me endlessly
 Bm7              E A/C# D
I am accepted by the God  I  serve        (rpt)
```

Verse 2:
I thought I would always seek You
Everyday I'd meet You, worship You with my whole life
But I found I'm weak and sometimes
My heart is divided, but I find You still love me

Bridge:
```
A      E/G#    A/G        D     A
Keep the wonder of Your grace in my mind
A      E/G#    A/G        D     A
Keep the wonder of Your grace in my mind
A      E/G#    A/G        D     G    E    D
Keep the wonder of Your grace in my mind
```

Taken from IS IT ANY WONDER
Heat
SURCD071

I'VE BEEN CAUGHT UP

Grace

James Gregory

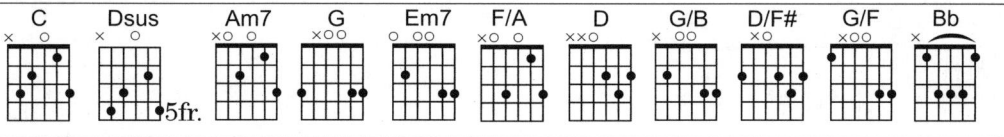

(Capo 2)

Intro: C   Dsus C   Dsus

Verse 1:
```
C                   Dsus     C
I've been caught up with so much and
   Dsus      C        Dsus       C       Dsus
I admit the love I had for You was growing cold
C           Dsus        C
I had filled my days with things that
     Dsus          C              Am7   Dsus    D
In the end don't matter, but I find You still love me
```

Chorus:
```
      G                        C          Em7
Your grace amazes me, You love me endlessly
 Am7   F/A          D G/B  C
I am accepted by the God  I  serve       (rpt)
```

Verse 2:
I thought I would always seek You
Everyday I'd meet You, worship You with my whole life
But I found I'm weak and sometimes
My heart is divided, but I find You still love me

Bridge:
```
G         D/F#     G/F      C        G
Keep the wonder of Your grace in my mind
G         D/F#     G/F      C        G
Keep the wonder of Your grace in my mind
G         D/F#     G/F      C        F   D   C
Keep the wonder of Your grace in my mind
```

Taken from IS IT ANY WONDER
Heat
SURCD071

The Overlap   Paul Oakley

Em7   C2   D   G   Asus

Intro: **Em7   C2   Em7   C2**
Verse 1:
Em7   D
   I've been searching for a city
           C2   Em7
One not built by the hands of man
                              D
And I've been looking for a country
         C2   Em7
A better place that I can call home
G   D
   I've been longing for a kingdom
        A7sus   C2
One I know is sure to come
Em7   D
   When the rider on the white horse
        C2   Em7
Comes again for His chosen ones   (to intro)

Verse 2:
Like a stranger in a strange land
I know I'm only passing through
It's so hard not to put my roots down, I'm trying to fix my eyes on You
The pleasures of this world may tempt me
But I've tasted something new
Like a pilgrim I will journey, I know I've set my hope on You

Chorus: **G   D**
I'm living in the overlap, I'm living in the balance
           C2   Em7
Between what is and is to come
              G   D
I'm living in freedom, but I'm caught in a tension
           C2   Em7
Between now and the age to come

Bridge:
Em7   G
   I don't want silver, don't want gold
A7sus   C2
   Or all the riches in this world
Em7   G
   Oh lover of my soul
   A7sus
In You are faithfulness and truth
   C2   C2
And all I need is found in You

Taken from UNAFRAID
Paul Oakley
SURCD081

I'VE COME TO YOU

Rex Allchurch

D	E	F#m7	E/G#	A

Intro: D E F#m7 E/G# A x2

Verse 1:
```
     A              E
I've come to You so many times
     F#m7           D
With songs that are just words
  A              D
I sing them through without the heart
     F#m7         D
But tell You they are true
```

Pre-Chorus:
```
    A              E
So help me God to live the life
     F#m7           D
That speaks through what I do
       A              E
That these are not just songs for church
     F#m7        D
But how I live for You
```

Verse 2:
```
I'll come back to the heart of why
These words are sung to You
I'll sing them through with all my heart
And live these words as truth
```

Chorus:
```
     D       E
So wash me now
     F#m7   E/G#     A
And make me more like You
 D          E
Cleanse my heart
 F#m7  E/G#     A
So I can worship You
```

Taken from
TO LOVE THE LOST
Rex Allchurch
RACD001

I'VE FILLED MY TIME
I Need To Get The Fire Back

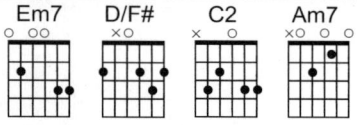

Matt Redman

Em7   D/F#   C2   Am7

Intro: Em7   D/F#   C2   D/F#

Verse 1:
    Em7
I've filled my time with preparations
D/F#
   Worn the cloak of endless serving
C2
  Though this is a part of loving
  Am7   D/F#
Something can grow cold
      Em7
I've wandered through this life's distractions
D/F#
   Clouding out my soul's attraction
C2
  When I take the time to listen
Am7   D/F#
  I can hear You call

Chorus:
Em7   D/F#   C2   D/F# Em7
  I need to get the fire   back
D/F# C2   D/F#
   Lord like the first time
Em7   D/F#   C2   D/F# Em7
  I need to get the fire   back
D/F# C2   D/F#
   You are my first love
Em7   D/F#   C2   D/F#   Em7
  The embers still remain
  D/F#   C2   D/F#
But Lord I miss the flame
Em7 D/F#   C2   D/F# Em7 D/F# C2 D/F#
  I need to get the fire   back

Verse 2:
Looking now upon the reason
I am living, I am breathing
Holy Father You are showing
All I need to know
I must take the time to listen
Not to know You from a distance
But to find in all Your nearness
You and You alone

Taken from FRIENDSHIP & THE FEAR
Matt Redman
SURCD001

I'VE HAD QUESTIONS

When The Tears Fall

Tim Hughes

Verse 1:
```
G                A        Bm7
I've had questions, without answers
G           Bm7          A
I've known sorrow, I have known pain
G                A        Bm7
But there's one thing, that I'll cling to
G           Bm7          A
You are faithful, Jesus You're true
```

Chorus:
```
G                D/F#        A
When hope is lost, I'll call You Saviour
G                D/F#        A
When pain surrounds,  I'll call You healer
G                Bm7         A              G
When silence falls,  You'll be the song within my heart
```

Verse 2:
```
In the lone hour of my sorrow
Through the darkest night of my soul
You surround me and sustain me
My defender, forever more
```

Bridge:
```
G           A         D/F#
I will praise You, I will praise You
G                A      D/F#
When the tears fall, still I will sing to You
G           A         D/F#
I will praise You, Jesus praise You
G                A      D/F#
Through the suffering still I will sing
```

JESUS CHRIST EMMANUEL

101

Martyn Layzell

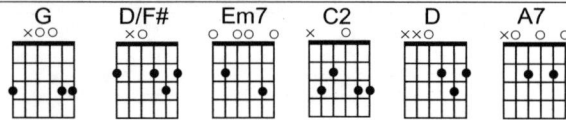

Intro: G   D/F#   Em7   C2   x2

Verse 1:
G   D/F# Em7   C2
Jesus Christ Emmanuel, Saviour of the world
G   D/F# Em7   C2
Creator of the universe, true and living Word
D/F#   C2
Let every tongue confess Your name
     D/F#   Em7   D/F#   C2
And bow the knee before Your hand of grace
                                    D
Giving You the highest praise

Chorus:
Em7   D/F#   G   C2
You are, You are the everlasting Prince of Peace
Em7   D/F#   G   D/F#
The first, the last, in whom all things were made
Em7   D/F#   G   A7
You reign in love, Counselor, Almighty God
C2   D   Em7   A7
Jesus You're the name by which we're saved
C2   D   (to intro)
Jesus You're the name by which we're saved

Verse 2:
Holy one upon the throne, to You the angels sing
Here we join their heavenly song, proclaiming You as King
Let every tongue confess Your name
And bow the knee before Your hand of grace
Giving You the highest praise

**Taken from
LOST IN WONDER
Martyn Layzell
SURCD076**

Copyright (c) 2001 Thankyou Music/Adm. by worshiptogether.com songs
excl. UK & Europe, adm. by Kingsway Music. tym@kingsway.co.uk Used by permission.

JESUS HOPE OF THE NATIONS

Hope Of The Nations

Brian Doerksen

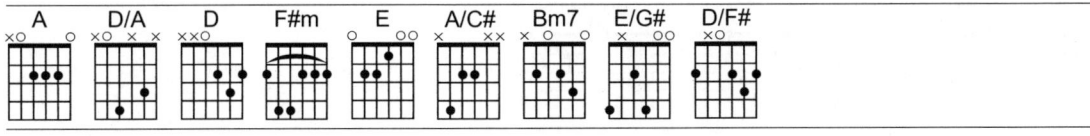

Verse 1:
```
A        D/A
  Jesus, hope of the nations
A         D                 F#m
  Jesus, comfort for all who mourn
      E            D              E
You are the source of heaven's hope on earth
```

Verse 2:
```
Jesus, light in the darkness
Jesus, truth in each circumstance
You are the source of heaven's light on earth
```

Pre-Chorus:
```
   D          A/C#
In history You lived and died
     Bm7
You broke the chains
     E
You rose to life
```

Chorus:
```
            A           D
You are the hope living in us
          E          A
You are the rock in whom we trust
     E/G# F#m         D         E    D/F#
You are the  light shining for all the world to see
                A           D
You rose from the dead conquering fear
            E          A
Our Prince of Peace drawing us near
     E/G# F#m         Bm7          E
Jesus our  hope living for all who will recieve
D          A    D    A    D
  Lord we believe
```

Taken from YOU SHINE
Brian Doerksen
Hosanna Music 22012

JESUS MY PASSION IN LIFE

Above All Else

Vicky Beeching

Chord diagrams: D, Bm7, Em7, D/F#, G, A7sus, D/G

Verse 1:

D   Bm7
Jesus my passion in life is to know You
                  Em7 D/F#
May all other goals bow down to
       G   A7sus   D
This journey of loving You more
 D   Bm7
Jesus You've showered Your goodness on me
             Em7 D/F#
Given Your gifts so free - ly
    G   A7sus   D
But there's one thing I'm longing for
Em7   D/F#
Hear my heart 's cry
       G   A7sus
And my prayer for this life

Chorus:
D/G   D/F#
  Above all else
Em7   A7sus
  Above all else
D/G   D/F#
  Above all else
Em7   A7sus   D
  Give me Yourself

Taken from HOLY
Vineyard Music UK
VMUKCD06

JESUS YOU ALONE

Tim Hughes

(no capo)

```
Intro:  B  F#/A#  G#m7  F#  E  B/D#  C#m7  F#sus
        B  F#/A#  G#m7  F#  E            F#sus
```

Verse 1:
```
B                         E
Jesus You alone shall be my first love
        F#
My first love
     B                             E
The secret place and highest praise shall be Yours
        F#
Shall be Yours
```

Pre-Chorus:
```
E       F#      G#m7    F#
To Your throne I'll bring devotion
E     F#    G#m7    F#
May it be the sweetest sound
E        F#     G#m7   F#    E    F#
Lord this heart is reaching for you now
```

Chorus:
```
B    F#/A#   G#m7    F#
So I'll set my sights upon You
E      B/D# C#m7       F#
Set my life upon Your praise
B    F#/A# G#m7    F#    E    F#
Never looking  to   another way
B    F#/A#   G#m7    F#
You alone will be my passion
E      B/D#   C#m7    F#
Jesus You will be my song
B        F#/A#    G#m7  F#   E   F#
You will find me longing after You
```

Verse 2:
Day and night I'll lift my eyes to seek You, to seek You
Hungry for a glimpse of You in glory, in glory

Taken from HERE I AM TO WORSHIP
Tim Hughes
SURCD053

JESUS YOU ALONE

Tim Hughes

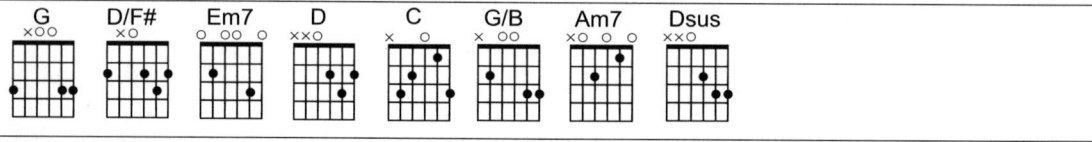

(Capo 4)

Intro: G D/F# Em7 D C G/B Am7 Dsus
           G D/F# Em7 D C   Dsus

Verse 1:
```
G                          C
Jesus You alone shall be my first love
        D
My first love
        G                                  C
The secret place and highest praise shall be Yours
        D
Shall be Yours
```

Pre-Chorus:
```
C         D       Em7       D
To Your throne I'll bring devotion
C         D       Em7       D
May it be the sweetest sound
C         D       Em7    D       C     D
Lord this heart is reaching for You now
```

Chorus:
```
G       D/F#   Em7      D
So I'll set my sights upon You
C       G/B   Am7          D
Set my life upon Your praise
G       D/F#   Em7      D       C    D
Never looking  to   another way
G       D/F#   Em7          D
You alone will be my passion
C       G/B    Am7       D
Jesus You will be my song
G       D/F#   Em7      D    C    D
You will find me longing after You
```

Verse 2:
Day and night I'll lift my eyes to seek You, to seek You
Hungry for a glimpse of You in glory, in glory

Taken from HERE I AM TO WORSHIP
Tim Hughes
SURCD053

JESUS YOU ARE

Thank You

Jeff Searles

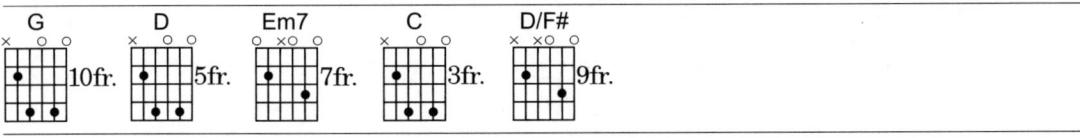

Intro: G D Em7 C x2

Verse:
G   D   Em7
  Jesus You are, and will always be
                     C
Beautiful and lovely to me
G   D   Em7
  You gave Your life, shed Your blood for me
                        C
Heaven came down to reveal Your love

Chorus:
 G   D/F#
Thank You, thank You
      Em7
I will always bring You praise
  C
You have won my heart
 G   D/F#
Thank You, thank You
      Em7
I will always bring You praise
        C
From the deepest places of my heart

Taken from
EVERYONE
EVRYONE
DPRO0119

One Thing I Long For   Herman Ypma

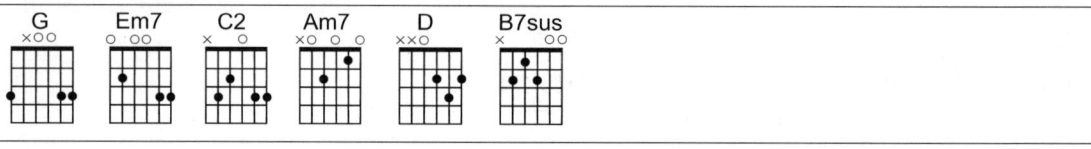

Intro: G   G   Em7   C2

Verse 1:
```
 G                              Em7            C2
Jesus, Your amazing grace just makes me want to sing
 G                              Em7            C2
Saviour, I am overwhelmed by all You've done for me
        Am7           D
You surrounded me with love
        Am7           D
All that held me fell away
        Em7              C2
In its place new life was given
        Am7           D
And I run to seek Your face
```


Chorus:
```
          G              Am7
Lord I long for more of You
 C2                    D
To be held close by Your side
          G              Am7
You have paid for me to come
          C2            D
And Your heart is open wide
          C2            D
To be carried near Your heart
        B7sus          Em7
To be found in Your embrace
             Am7
One thing I long for
          D              G
To be close to You each day
```

Taken from the
INTERNATIONAL PEOPLE'S ALBUM
Soul Survivor
SURCD054

JESUS, JESUS

Shine In Glory

Ben Wilkes

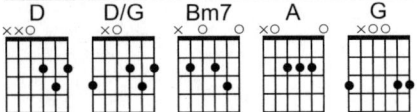

Verse 1:
D D/G   D D/G
Jesus, Jesus
       Bm7   A   G
Bend to kiss   One who saves
D D/G   D D/G
Jesus, Jesus
        Bm7   A   G
I rest my soul   in Your arms

Chorus:
        D A
Shine in glory
        G D
Shine in glory
        Bm7 A   G
Shine in glo - ry, please

Verse 2:
Jesus, Jesus
I submit all to You

Taken from
BIOGRAPHY
Revelation Warehouse
SURCD079

Redeemer

(no capo)

Intro: F   Am7   Bb   x2

Verse 1:
```
F      Am7    Bb
Jesus    Redeemer
F           Am7      Bb
Friend and King to me
        F   Am7    Bb
My refuge    My comfort
           F   Am7    Bb
You're everything to me
          Gm7        Am7      Bb
And this heart is on fire for You
          Gm7        Am7      Bb
Yes this heart is on fire for You
```

Chorus:
```
      F                       Dm7
For You alone are wonderful, You alone are counsellor
Gm7        F/A      Bb           Csus
Everlasting Father, mighty in the heavens
   F                   Dm7
Never to forget the love You displayed upon a cross
Gm7        F/A        Bb            Csus         F
Son of God I thank You, Prince of Peace I love Your name
```

Verse 2:
Saviour, Healer, just and true are You
Now reigning in glory, most high and living God
This heart is in awe of You
Yes this heart is in awe of You

Taken from HERE I AM TO WORSHIP
Tim Hughes
SURCD053

JESUS, REDEEMER

Redeemer

E   G#m7   A2   Bsus   F#m7

(Capo 1)

Intro: E   G#m7   A2   x2

Verse 1:
E   G#m7   A2
Jesus,   Redeemer
    E   G#m7   A2
Friend and King to me
        E   G#m7   A2
My refuge,   My comfort
            E   G#m7   A2
You're everything to me
          F#m7   G#m7   A2
And this heart is on fire for You
          F#m7   G#m7   A2
Yes this heart is on fire for You

Chorus:
        E   C#m7
For You alone are wonderful, You alone are counselor
F#m7   E/G#   A2   Bsus
Everlasting Father, mighty in the heavens
    E   C#m7
Never to forget the love You displayed upon a cross
F#m7   E/G#   A2   Bsus   E
Son of God I thank You, Prince of Peace I love Your name

Verse 2:
Saviour, Healer, just and true are You
Now reigning in glory, most high and living God
This heart is in awe of You
Yes this heart is in awe of You

Taken from HERE I AM TO WORSHIP
Tim Hughes
SURCD053

JESUS SAVIOUR

109

Jeff Searles

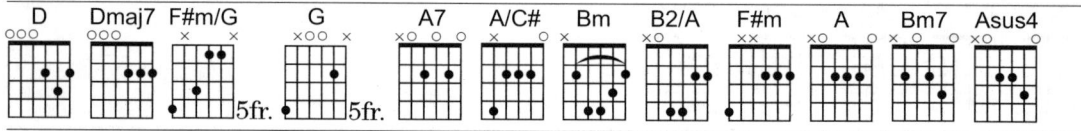

D Dmaj7 F#m/G G A7 A/C# Bm B2/A F#m A Bm7 Asus4

(Tune Low E string down to D)

Verse 1:
```
D        Dmaj7   D       Dmaj7      F#m/G  G  F#m/G  G
Jesus, Saviour, how can I ever be the  same?
A7                                 D  Dmaj7  D  Dmaj7
I have felt love's touch, softer than the rain
D        Dmaj7   D        Dmaj7             F#m/G  G  F#m/G  G
Jesus, Saviour, symphony of praise surrounds Your  name
A7                                 D  Dmaj7  D  A/C#
Angels sing Your praise as You rule and reign
```

Chorus:
```
    Bm     B2/A      G
No higher praise has a king heard
F#m     G        D      A
Than the Christ who died for us
        Bm        B2/A       G
You deserve the anthem of our  praise
F#m     G      D      A    D
We will live to worship only You
```

Verse 2:
```
I have heard a song that whispers through the trees at night
Bringing hope and love like a lullaby
I have found a peace in You, a peace that lets me go
To a place of life purer than the snow
```

Bridge:
```
D      A/C#    Bm7     Asus4              G      Asus4  A    D
Jesus, Saviour, Prince of Peace, You are the door unto      the sheep
D      A/C#  Bm7     Asus4         G      Asus4  A    D
Son of God, living sacrifice, You are the light of      the world      (repeat)
```

Taken from
EVERYONE
EVERYONE
DPRO0119

JUST LIKE THE ONES

We Will Go

Brenton Brown

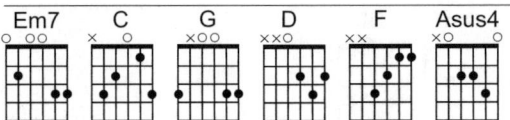

Em7   C   G   D   F   Asus4

Verse 1:
        Em7   C
Just like the ones who came before us
        G   D
Just like the ones who gave their lives
        Em7   C
Lord we will leave this place with You
        G   D
And we will go, we will go
        Em7   C
Just as You came to earth from heaven
        G   D
Humbled Yourself, gave Your life
        Em7   C
We want to follow and obey You
        G   D
So we will go, we will go

Chorus:
        G   D
Light of the world, You shone on us
          F   C
You filled our hearts with hope that reaches out
        G   D
Friend of the world, Saviour to me
         F   C   Em7 C G D
Make me a flame, set me on fire to be a light in the world

Verse 2:
Just as they prayed to You for power
That they'd be bold to speak Your Word
Father we ask that You would fill us
As we go, as we go
Just as they asked You for salvation
Just as they prayed for kingdom signs
Lord would You send us with Your Spirit
       G   Asus4   C
As we go, as we go,   we want to go

Tag:
        Em7   C
Set me on fire Lord make me a flame
        G   D (Asus4   C)
Release revival please do it again   (Lord do it again)
                    (last time)

Taken from
ON THE STREETS
Festival Manchester 2003
SURCD095

KING JESUS I BELIEVE

Martyn Layzell

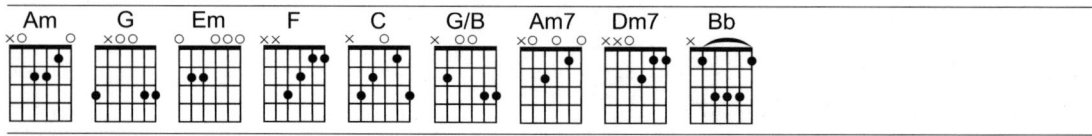

Verse 1:
Am   G   Em   F
   King Jesus I believe the words of life You breathe
Am   G   Em   F
You've spoken promises, a guiding light for our feet
Am   G   Em   F
   We fall down to our knees and weep with those who weep
   Em   F   G
Let justice flow upon this earth, a never failing stream

Chorus:
     C   G/B   Am7   F
I'm thirsty,   longing just to see Your kingdom come
C   G/B   Am7 F
Praying that today Your love is shown
     C   G/B   Am7   F
I'm thirsty,   for the will of God to be made known
C   G/B   Am7 F
Praying for the day of Your return

Verse 2:
You have anointed us to bind the broken heart
Proclaim deliverance for those enslaved in the dark
You pour the oil of joy all over my despair
O Spirit of the sovereign Lord empower us once again

Bridge:
Dm7   Bb   C   Am7
   We pray,   we pray, we seek Your face
Dm7   Bb   G
   We pray,   we seek Your face   (repeat)

Taken from
LOST IN WONDER
Martyn Layzell
SURCD076

LIGHT OF THE WORLD

Here I Am To Worship

Tim Hughes

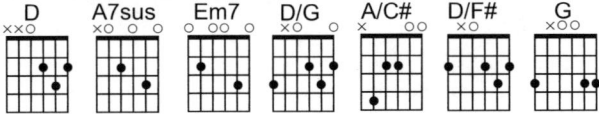

D	A7sus	Em7	D/G	A/C#	D/F#	G

(Capo 2)

Verse 1:
E (D)   B (A7sus)
Light of the world
            F#m7 (Em7)
You stepped down into darkness
E (D)   B (A7sus)
Opened my eyes
       E/A (D/G)
Let me see
E (D)   B (A7sus)
Beauty that made
      F#m7 (Em7)
This heart adore You
E (D)   B (Asus)   E/A (D/G)
Hope of a life spent with You

Chorus:
           E (D)   B/D# (A/C#)
So here I am to worship, here I am to bow down
        E/G# (D/F#)   A (G)
Here I am to say that You're my God
          E (D)   B/D# (A/C#)
You're altogether lovely, altogether worthy
        E/G# (D/F#)   A (G)
Altogether wonderful to me

Verse 2:
King of all days, oh so highly exalted
Glorious in heaven above
Humbly You came to the earth You created
All for love's sake became poor

Bridge:
      B/D# (A/C#)   E/G# (D/F#)   A (G)
And I'll never   know how much it cost
  B/D# (A/C#)   E/G# (D/F#)   A (G)
To see my   sin   upon that cross

Taken from HERE I AM TO WORSHIP
Tim Hughes
SURCD053

LIKE A FRAGRANT OIL

Fragrant

Paul Oakley

C2   G/B   Am7   F

(Capo 4)

Verse 1:
E (C2)   B/D# (G/B)
  Like a fragrant oil
C#m7 (Am7)   A (F)
     Like costly perfume poured out
E (C2)   B/D# (G/B)   C#m7 (Am7)   A (F)
  Let my worship be to You
E (C2)   B/D# (G/B)
  Like a fervent prayer
C#m7 (Am7)   A (F)
     Like incense rising to Your throne
E (C2) B/D# (G/B)   C#m7 (Am7)   A (F)
   In spirit and in truth

Chorus:
  E (C2)   B/D# (G/B)   C#m7 (Am7)
Jesus
              A (F)
You alone are worthy of my praise
E (C2) B/D# (G/B)   C#m7 (Am7) A (F)
 I owe my life to You
  E (C2)   B/D# (G/B)   C#m7 (Am7)
Jesus
              A (F)
You alone can make me holy
E (C2) B/D# (G/B)   C#m7 (Am7) A (F)
 So I bow before You

Verse 2:
Like a wedding vow
"All I am I give to You"
Let my sacrifice be pure
Like the sweetest sound
Like a lover's whisper in your ear
I've set my heart on You

Taken from UNAFRAID
Paul Oakley
SURCD081

LOOKING AT MY LIFE

All That I Am

Hope Turner

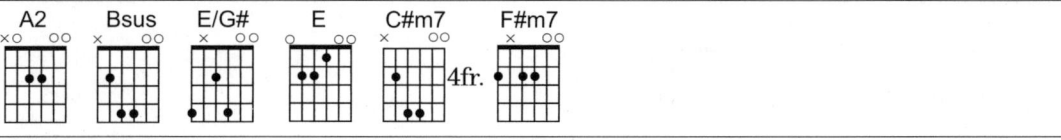

A2   Bsus   E/G#   E   C#m7   F#m7

Verse 1:
A2   Bsus   E/G#
Looking at my life I think of all You've done
A2   Bsus   E
You build me up when I fall down
A2   Bsus   E/G#
Looking at the world I can see Your face
A2   Bsus   E
You're all I need

Pre-Chorus:
C#m7   Bsus   A2
So please don't turn away from me
          C#m7   Bsus   A2
I need to see Your beauty Lord

Chorus:
        A2 Bsus   E
I give You all that I am
              A2 Bsus   E
For You have given life to me
          A2   Bsus
In every breath that I take
        E
Each moment I'm awake
 F#m7
I live to serve my King

Verse 2:
I live to worship You as long as I live
Lord take Your praise
I will worship You in Spirit and in truth
You're all I need

LORD I COME TO YOU

How Can I Do Anything But Praise You?

Colse Leung

C   G/B   Am7   F   G   Em7

(Capo 5)

Verse:
F (C)
Lord I come to You
  C/E (G/B)
Broken and lost
Dm7 (Am7)   Bb (F)
Jesus be the highest part
F (C)
Here I am again
  C/E (G/B)
Longing for more
Dm7 (Am7)   Bb (F)
Waiting for Your presence here
                    C (G)
Your presence here

Chorus:
F (C)
How can I do anything but praise You?
Am7 (Em7)
How can I not worship You?
    Dm7 (Am7)   C (G)   Bb (F)
And how can I live my life without You God?
F (C)
Lord You amaze me with Your favour
Am7 (Em7)
Lord You astound me with Your love
    Dm7 (Am7)   C (G)   Bb (F)
And how can I live my life without You God?

Taken from the
INTERNATIONAL PEOPLE'S ALBUM
Soul Survivor
SURCD054

LORD I'M GRATEFUL

Grace

Stuart Townend & Fred J Heumann

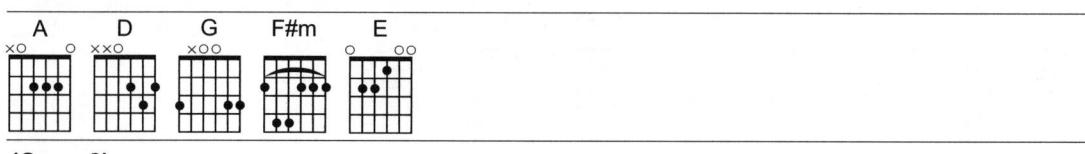

(Capo 2)

Verse 1:
B (A)   E (D)   B (A)   E (D)
Lord I'm grateful, amazed at what You've done
B (A)   E (D)   A (G) E (D)
  My finest efforts are filthy rags
    B (A)   E (D)   B (A)   E (D)
But I'm made righteous by trusting in the Son
B (A)   E (D)   A (G)   E (D)
  I have God's riches at Christ's expense

Chorus:
        B (A)   E (D)   B (A) E (D)   B (A)
'Cause it's grace there's nothing I can do to make You love me more
 E (D)   A (G)   E (D)
To make You love me less than You do
     B (A)   E (D)   B (A)   E (D)   B (A)
And by faith I'm standing on this stone of Christ and Christ alone
 E (D)   A (G)   E (D)
Your righteousness is all that I need
        B (A)
'Cause it's grace

Verse 2:
Called and chosen when I was far away
You brought me into Your family
Free forgiven my guilt is washed away
Your loving kindness is life to me

Bridge:
G#m (F#m)
Grace loves the sinner
    E (D)   B (A) E (D)
Loves all I am and all I'll ever be
G#m (F#m)
Makes me a winner
    E (D)   A (G) F# (E)
Whatever lies the devil throws at me

Verse 3:
Freely given but bought with priceless blood
My life was ransomed at Calvary
There my Jesus gave everything He could
That I might live for eternity

Taken from
LORD OF EVERY HEART
Stuart Townend
KMCD2404

LORD LET YOUR GLORY FALL

You Are Good

Matt Redman

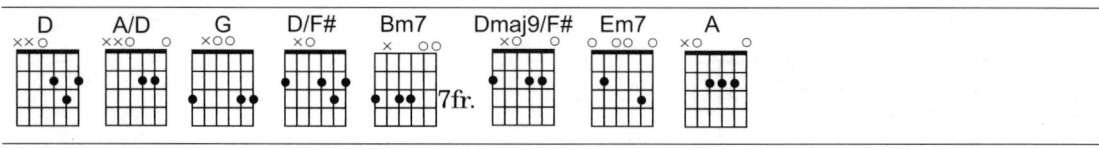

Verse 1:
```
D       A/D      G D/F#              G
Lord let Your glory fall as on that ancient day
Bm7      Dmaj7/F# G  Em7           G     D
Songs of enduring love, and then Your glory came
 D       A/D      G   D/F#              G
And as a sign to You that we would love the same
Bm7      Dmaj7/F#        G   Em7        G       D
Our hearts will sing that song, God let Your glory come
```

Chorus:
```
        D/F#                      G
You are good, You are good and Your love endures
        D/F#                      G
You are good, You are good and Your love endures
        Bm7          D/F#      G              D
You are good, You are good and Your love endures today
```

Verse 2:
```
D      A/D    G   D/F#                  G
Voices in unison giving You thanks and praise
 Bm7   Dmaj7/F#   G   Em7          G     D
Joined by the instruments, and then Your glory came
 D      A/D       G   D/F#              G
Your presence like a cloud upon that ancient day
Bm7      Dmaj7/F#       G     Em7        G     D
The priests were overwhelmed because Your glory came
```

Verse 3:
```
A sacrifice was made and then Your fire came
They knelt upon the ground and with one voice they praised
```

Tag:
```
      Bm7
Your anger lasts a moment
              G           D    A
But Your favour lasts a lifetime
```

Taken from
WHERE ANGELS FEAR TO TREAD
Matt Redman
SURCD074

LORD OF ALL CREATION

God Of Wonders

Marc Byrd & Steve Hindalong

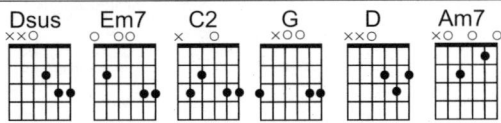

Dsus Em7 C2 G D Am7

(Capo 1)

Verse 1:
```
Dsus          Em7  C2
    Lord  of  all creation
Dsus          Em7       C2
    Of water earth and sky
Dsus                    Em7  C2
    The heavens are Your tabernacle
Dsus          Em7       C2
    Glory to the Lord on high
```

Chorus:
```
 G                             D
God of wonders beyond our galaxy
         Am7   C2
You are holy,  holy
         G                     D
The universe declares Your majesty
         Am7   C2
You are holy,  holy
C2
Lord of heaven and earth
C2                   Dsus  Em7  C2
Lord of heaven and earth
```

Tag:
```
Am7               C2              Am7
    Hallelujah to the Lord of heaven and earth
                  C2              Am7
Hallelujah to the Lord of heaven and earth
                  C2              G
Hallelujah to the Lord of heaven and earth
```

Taken from WORSHIP GOD
Rebecca St James
FFD32587

LORD THIS HEART MUST SING

Never Lose The Wonder

Tim Hughes

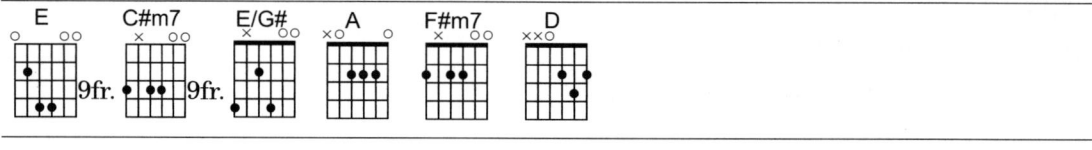

(Capo 1)

Intro: F (E)   Dm7 (C#m7)   F/A (E/G#)   Bb (A)   x2

Verse 1:
Dm7 (C#m7)   F (E)
Lord this heart must sing
                              Bb (A)
Of all that You have done for me
Dm7 (C#m7)   F (E)
The beauty of the cross
                              Bb (A)
The greatness of Your loss
      Gm7 (F#m7) F/A (E/G#)   Bb (A)
So I'll thank You   for the day
         Gm7 (F#m7) F/A (E/G#)   Eb (D)
When You washed my   sin   away

Chorus:
         F (E)   Dm7 (C#m7)
I will never lose the wonder
      F/A (E/G#)   Bb (A)
Of the blood You shed for me
               F (E)   Dm7 (C#m7)
There could be no greater love than this
      F/A (E/G#)   Bb (A)
Through all   eternity
      Gm7 (F#m7) F/A (E/G#)   Bb (A)
So I'll thank You   for the day
         Gm7 (F#m7) F/A (E/G#)   Eb (D)
When You washed my   sin   away

Verse 2:
Help me understand
Just what it meant for You, Jesus
The holy king of all
Upon a sinner's cross
So I'll thank You for the day
When You washed my sin away

Taken from HERE I AM TO WORSHIP
Tim Hughes
SURCD053

LORD YOU ARE MORE BEAUTIFUL

120

Walk

Simon Paylor

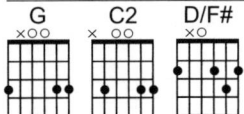

Verse 1:
G   C2
Lord, You are more beautiful than I could know
G   C2
Lord, You are more tender than I've ever known
D/F#   C2
Lord, You are more faithful than I'll ever know

Chorus:
   C2   G
I give my life to You
                  C2
I will walk with You
                  G
I give my life to You
                  C2
I will walk with You

Verse 2:
Lord, You are worth so much more than anything
Lord, You are higher than everything
Lord, You have power over everything

Verse 3:
Lord, You love me more than I could know
Lord, You embrace and hold me safe, I know
Lord, You, You long for me to be with You

Bridge:
G   C2
Watching, waiting, hoping, longing for You
G   C2
Watching, waiting, hoping, longing for You
G   C2
Watching, waiting, hoping, longing for You
G   C2
Watching, waiting, hoping, longing for You

Taken from
BIOGRAPHY
Revelation Warehouse
SURCD079

LORD YOU'RE NEAR

Samuel Lane

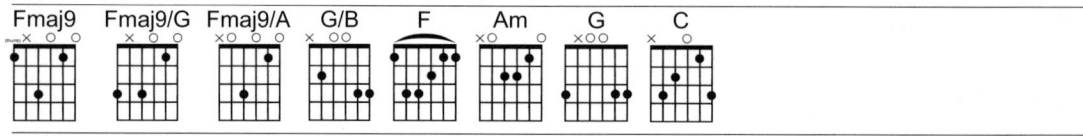

Intro: Fmaj9   Fmaj9/G   Fmaj9/A   G/B

Verse 1:
Fmaj9   Fmaj9/G Fmaj9/A   G/B
     Lord You're near to those who are discouraged
Fmaj9   Fmaj9/G   Fmaj9/A G/B
     You save those who have lost all hope
Fmaj9   Fmaj9/G   Fmaj9/A   G/B
     You've taken my sorrow, and surrounded me with joy
Fmaj9   Fmaj9/G Fmaj9/A   G/B
     You're here with me, Your touch gives me life

Chorus:
F   Am
  To You, O Lord
         G   F
Must the glory be given
F   Am
  To You, O Lord
         G   F
Must the glory be given   (repeat)

Verse 2:
Lord You're near, I feel secure, nothing can take me
I know Your love will be with me for all time
O Lord, You know what I long for
You're all I want in this life, don't leave me

Bridge:
F   G   Am   C   G
  Praise Him, praise Him, praise Him, praise Him
       F   G   Am   F   G
Praise Him, praise Him, praise Him, praise Him, praise Him

Taken from
BEAUTIFUL
Burn : UK
VMUKCD07

MAY THE WORDS OF MY MOUTH

Tim Hughes & Rob Hill

Verse 1:
```
      C            G/B
May the words of my mouth
         Am7         G
And the thoughts of my heart
           F        C    G
Bless Your name, bless Your name Jesus
         C         G/B
And the deeds of the day
         Am7        G
And the truth in my way
           F        C   G
Speak of You speak of You Jesus
```

Chorus:
```
         C              F
For this is what I'm glad to do
         Am7      Am7/G         D/F#    G
It's time to live a life of love that pleases You
         C             F
And I will give my all to You
         Am7      Am7/G         D/F#    G
Surrender everything I have and follow You
         F
I'll follow You
```

Verse 2:
Lord will You be my vision
Lord will You be my guide
Be my hope, be my light and the way
And I'll look not for riches
Or praises on earth
Only You'll be the first of my heart

Bridge:
```
Am7    G/B C          D  Am7   G/B C          D
I will follow,  I will follow You, I will follow,  I will follow You
Am7    G/B C          D  Am7   G/B C          D   F
I will follow,  I will follow You, I will follow,  I will follow You
```

Taken from HERE I AM TO WORSHIP
Tim Hughes
SURCD053

MY GOD IS FOR ME

For Me

Alan Rose

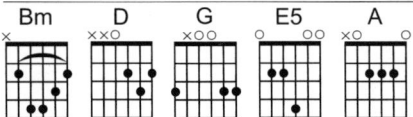

```
Bm      D       G      E5      A
```

Verse 1:

```
            Cm (Bm)
My God is for me
Eb (D)                      Ab (G)
  I know His hand is on my life
F5 (E5)      Bb (A)        Cm (Bm)
  I have the blessing of the Father
Eb (D)                      Ab (G)
  A sweet assurance in my heart
F5 (E5)  Bb (A)  Cm (Bm)
  That  I'm forgiven
Eb (D)                      Ab (G)
  No condemnation now for me
F5 (E5)   Bb (A)          Cm (Bm)
  In  Jesus Christ I am accepted
Eb (D)                 Ab (G)
  I am a son and I am free
```

Chorus:

```
F5 (E5)  Bb (A)  Ab (G)                   Cm (Bm)
   So  tell me who can separate me from His love?
Ab (G)                       Cm (Bm)        Bb (A)
Who can snatch me from His hand or stand against His perfect plan?
   Ab (G)                     Cm (Bm)
For I am hidden now with Christ in God
           Ab (G)              F5 (E5)    Bb (A)
Secure for eternity, secure in His love
```

Verse 2:

```
I have been lifted
Out of the mire to the rock
I have been made alive with Jesus
The old has gone, the new has come
And now I'm living
In all the blessing that You've won
Your Holy Spirit is my helper
I know I'll always be Your son
```

MY HEART IS SET

Holding Me

James Gregory

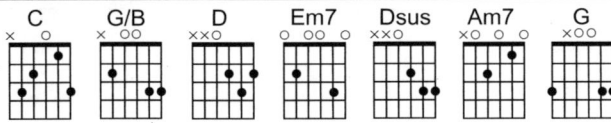

C   G/B   D   Em7   Dsus   Am7   G

Intro: C G D Em7 C G Dsus D

C G D Em7 Am7 D G

Verse 1:
```
    Em7          D    C    Em7        D  C
My heart is set to follow You as closely as I can
    Em7        D      C    Em7    D  C
To not let compromising color me
        Em7        D    C      Em7         D    C
But sometimes I am disobedient, sometimes just a fool
    G/B              C         Dsus  D
But You won't let this fire die in me
```

Chorus:
```
    C          G/B            D          Em7
I know You're holding me and will not let me go
    C    G/B            Dsus    D
I can't exhaust Your love for me
    C    G/B        D          Em7
I find security in knowing that I'm known
Am7      G/B        C          D      G
I am so grateful that You are so faithful to me
```

Verse 2:
Let me be a wise believer always learning more
Growing in maturity and faith
Teach me in the day to day more of who You are
Help me make my whole life into praise

Taken from IS IT ANY WONDER
Heat
SURCD071

MY HEART YEARNS

Greater Revelation

David Gate

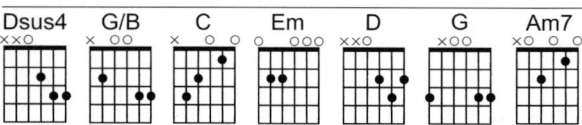

Intro: Dsus4 G/B C x4

Verse 1:
C
My heart yearns for something pure
     Em
For something true
C
My soul longs to know You Lord
     Em
For more of You
             C   D
A deeper understanding
          C   D
A greater revelation

Chorus:
G   Am7
Lead us to that Holy Place
G/B   C
Far beyond the outer courts
  G   Am7
To meet You where Your glory dwells
    G/B   C
And see a greater revelation

Verse 2:
C   Em
Emmanuel, Christ with us, here today
    C
On holy ground, Your presence now
    Em
O Lord we pray
                C   D
For a deeper sense of wonder
          C   D
A greater revelation

Tag:
        Dsus4   G/B   C
Show us more...

MY JESUS, MY LIFELINE

Tim Hughes

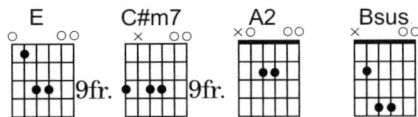

Verse 1:
E   C#m7
My Jesus, my lifeline
A2   Bsus
I need You more than I've ever known
E   C#m7
There's no one quite like You
A2   Bsus
I'm crying out for Your loving

Chorus:
A2 C#m7   A2
Oh Jesus, oh Jesus
            C#m7   Bsus   A2
I've never known a love like this before
     C#m7   A2
Oh Jesus, sweet Jesus
       C#m7 Bsus   A2
Accept this love I give to You
            E
It's all I can do

Verse 2:
I'm searching, I'm longing
Please meet me just as You want to
I'll stand here to offer
Offer up this song of love to You

Taken from HERE I AM TO WORSHIP
Tim Hughes
SURCD053

NO OTHER LOVE

Angie Weeks

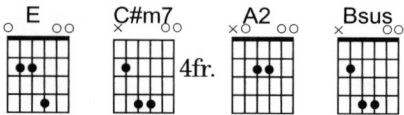

Verse 1:
```
E          A2                  E            Bsus
```
No other love can change my life the way that You have O Lord
```
C#m7                      Bsus
```
No other touch can find this deep and secret place of my heart
```
E          A2                  E       Bsus
```
No other friend could be so faithful, so pure and so true
```
C#m7                  Bsus
```
No other god, no other love, no other saviour but You

Chorus:
```
E
```
La da da dey
```
              A2
```
I can see You now
```
            Bsus
```
La da da dey
```
                  E
```
I can see You now   (rpt)

Taken from the
INTERNATIONAL PEOPLE'S ALBUM
Soul Survivor
SURCD054

NO WORDS

(no capo)

Intro: B : Bmaj7   B : Bmaj7   C#m7   F#6   x2

Verse 1:
```
B      C#m7                  F#     C#m7      F#
```
No words could speak of the depth of the love that's in You
```
B      C#m7             F#        C#m7      F#
```
No songs could put into words the hope that's found in You
```
G#m7       F#              E  F#
```
Through it all I'm following Jesus
```
       C#m7 F#             E  F#
```
Resting in Jesus, living for Jesus

Chorus:
```
B         Bmaj7  B        Bmaj7
```
You know I'll fall, but I'll sing through it all
```
C#m7           F#
```
Hey yeah, You know I love You
```
B      Bmaj7         B         Bmaj7
```
Rain falls, wind comes, when it's all said and done
```
C#m7             F#           G
```
Hey yeah, You know I love You
```
F#7                              to intro
```
You know I love You / I L.O.V.E You

Verse 2:
I won't let brokenness stop me 'cause I long for Your presence
I won't let other things blind me, I long to see You
Through it all I'm following Jesus
Resting in Jesus, living for Jesus

Taken from CLOSE TO YOU
Johnny Parks
SURCD055

NO WORDS

Johnny Parks

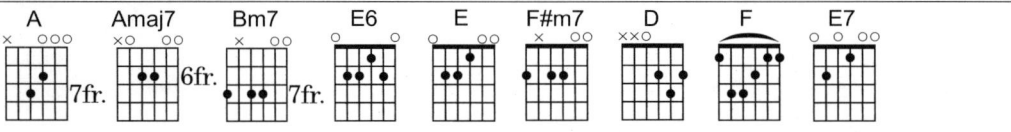

(Capo 2)

Intro: A : Amaj7 A : Amaj7 Bm7 E6   x2

Verse 1:
```
A       Bm7              E     Bm7      E
No words could speak of the depth of the love that's in You
A       Bm7              E     Bm7      E
No songs could put into words the hope that's found in You
 F#m7      E           D  E
Through it all I'm following Jesus
         Bm7  E          D  E
Resting in Jesus, living for Jesus
```

Chorus:
```
A     Amaj7    A       Amaj7
You know I'll fall, but I'll sing through it all
Bm7          E6
Hey yeah, You know I love You
A     Amaj7        A        Amaj7
Rain falls, wind comes, when it's all said and done
Bm7          E6           F
Hey yeah, You know I love You
 E7                         to intro
You know I love You / I L.O.V.E You
```

Verse 2:
I won't let brokenness stop me 'cause I long for Your presence
I won't let other things blind me, I long to see You
Through it all I'm following Jesus
Resting in Jesus, living for Jesus

Taken from CLOSE TO YOU
Johnny Parks
SURCD055

NOT BY WORDS

You Opened Up My Eyes

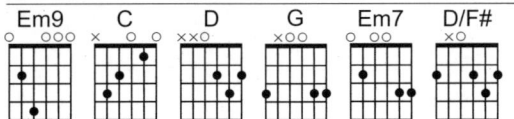

Em9   C   D   G   Em7   D/F#

(Capo 2)

Verse 1:

```
      F#m9 (Em9)        D (C)
Not by words and not by deeds
      F#m9 (Em9)        D (C)
But by grace we have been  saved
      F#m9 (Em9)   D (C)         E (D)
And it is the gift of God, the faith we need
      F#m9 (Em9)        D (C)
Not by strength and not by might
      F#m9 (Em9)   D (C)
But with power from on  high
      F#m9 (Em9)   D (C)         E (D)      D (C)
So that we can only boast, boast in You
```

Chorus:

```
A (G)            D (C)         E (D)
   For once I was dead now I'm alive
   D(C)              A (G)
For freedom I'm set free
              D (C)          E (D)
And in Your great love, I have found life
      D(C)           A (G)
You opened up my eyes
```

Verse 2:

```
Not with eloquence or fame
But in weakness and in shame
For the power of Your strength is then revealed
And the message of Your cross
Seems like foolishness to some
But the mercy of Your grace is hidden there
```

Bridge:

```
F#m7 (Em7)      E/G# (D/F#)     A (G)          D (C)
   What mercy,      what mercy,  what mercy beneath the cross
F#m7 (Em7)      E/G# (D/F#)     A (G)          D (C)
   What mercy,      what mercy,  what mercy beneath the cross
F#m7 (Em7)      E/G# (D/F#)     A (G)          D (C)
   Your mercy,      Your mercy,  Your mercy beneath the cross
F#m7 (Em7)      E/G# (D/F#)     A (G)          D (C)
   Your mercy,      Your mercy,  Your mercy beneath the cross
```

Taken from
LOST IN WONDER
Martyn Layzell
SURCD076

O FALLEN ONE

Arise And Shine

James Gregory

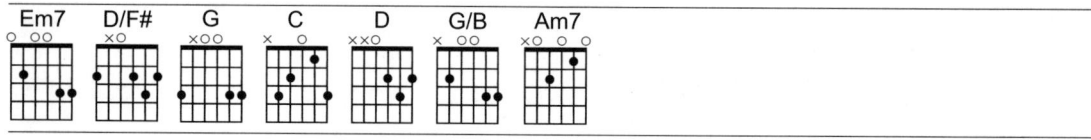

Verse 1:
Em7   D/F# G
    O fallen one covered now in shame
Em7   D/F#   C
    He is your hope, He is your life
Em7   D/F#   G
    Though He should judge His anger turns away
Em7   D/F#   C
    Rise from the dust beautiful one

Verse 2:
Don't be afraid for you're not left alone
His heart of love is broken for You
Your Father cares for all your children now
Arise in His name beautiful one

Chorus:
  C   D   G/B C   D
Arise and shine your glory has come
G/B C   D   G/B C   D
 Arise and shine your glory has come
 Am7   Em7   C   D
Arise and shine, He is calling You by name
          Am7   Em7
Though your walls have fallen down
          C
He'll build you up again

Verse 3:
Lift up your eyes, many come to see
The splendour your God has given to You
Could each of Your saints become a thousand saints
Rise up and praise beautiful one

Bridge:
D/F# Em7   C   D   D/F#   Em7 C
 So let Your salvation come for Your glory Lord
D/F# Em7   C   D   D/F#   Em7   C
 Set the captives free we pray, these souls are Your reward

Taken from
ON THE STREETS
Festival Manchester 2003
SURCD095

O GOD OF LOVE

131

How Good It Is

Louise & Nathan Fellingham

G Am7 C2 C/D Em7 G/B D

Capo 2

Verse 1:
G   Am7   C2   C/D
 O God of love, I come to You again
G   Am7   C2
  Knowing I'll find mercy
G Am7   C2 C/D   Em7
 I can't explain all the things I see
          G/B   Am7
But I'll trust in You
G/B C2   G/B
 In every moment You are there
  C2   G/B   D
Watching over You hear my prayer
    Am7   Em7
You go before me, You're behind me
C2   D
Nothing's hidden from You

Chorus:
G   Am7 C2 C/D
  How good it is   to be loved by You
G   Am7 C2 C/D
  How good it is
G   Am7 C2 C/D
  How good it is   to be loved by You
G   Am7 C2 C/D
  How good it is

Verse 2:
O God of strength, Your hand is on my life
Bringing peace to me
You know my frame, You know how I am made
You planned all my days
Hand of mercy, hand of love, giving power to overcome
If all beneath me falls away, I know that You are God

Middle 8:
Em7   G/B   C2
Who can stand against us?
      Em7   G/B   C2
In my weakness You are strong
      Em7   G/B   C2
Your word is ever - lasting
      Em7   G/B   Am7   G/B C2
I will praise You faithful One

Taken from
CHOSEN FROM THE NATIONS
Stoneleigh Live Worship 2000
KMCD2288

How Good It Is

Louise & Nathan Fellingham

Verse 1:
A　Bm7　　D2　　D/E
　O God of love, I come to You again
A　　　　Bm7　　D2
　　Knowing I'll find mercy
A　Bm7　　D2　D/E　　　　　　F#m7
　I can't explain all the things I see
　　　　　A/C#　　Bm7
But I'll trust in You
A/C# D　　　　　　　A2/C#
　In　every moment You are there
　　D　　　　　　　A/C#　　　E
Watching over You hear my prayer
　　Bm7　　　　　F#m7
You go before me, You're behind me
D　　　　　　　　　　E
Nothing's hidden from You

Chorus:
A　　　Bm7　　D2 D/E
　How good it　is　to be loved by You
A　　　Bm7　　D2　D/E
　How good it is
A　　　Bm7　　D2 D/E
　How good it　is　to be loved by You
A　　　Bm7　　D2　D/E
　How good it　is

Verse 2:
O God of strength, Your hand is on my life
Bringing peace to me
You know my frame, You know how I am made
You planned all my days
Hand of mercy, hand of love, giving power to overcome
If all beneath me falls away, I know that You are God

Middle 8:
F#m7　　A/C#　　　D
Who can stand against us?
　　　F#m7　　A/C#　　　D
In my weakness You are strong
　　　F#m7　A/C#　D
Your word is ever - lasting
　　　F#m7　　　A/C#　Bm7　　A/C# D
I will praise You faithful One

Taken from
CHOSEN FROM THE NATIONS
Stoneleigh Live Worship 2000
KMCD2288

O LORD I AM DEVOTED

Devoted

Martyn Layzell

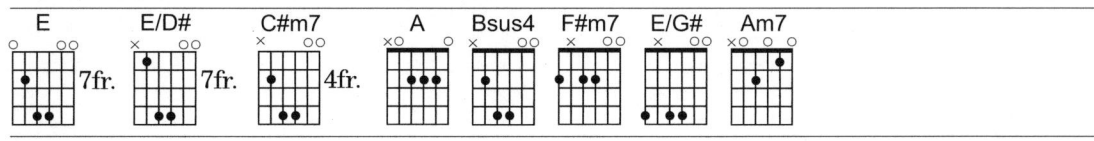

Verse 1:
```
E                        E/D#
O Lord I am devoted to You
                  C#m7
All that I am I give You
                 A        Bsus4
Nothing do I withhold
E
I am nothing without You
E/D#
All my hope is upon You
C#m7                    A
Simply telling You I am Yours
    F#m7        Bsus4
I am Yours
```

Chorus:
```
E                           E/G#
Jesus may my devotion be pleasing
                            F#m7
Expressed through this song I am singing
                   Am7      F#m7     Bsus4
I'm pouring my heart out to You, only You
E                          E/G#
You are the reason I'm living and breathing
                        F#m7
My refuge, my strength and my healing
                 Am7     F#m7    Bsus4    E
So I give my heart unto You, only You
```

Verse 2:
Every earthly distraction
Fades away to the background
I'm content just to be with You
Jesus You satisfy my longing
To You do I cry, I'm coming
Kneeling before Your throne
At Your throne

Taken from
LOST IN WONDER
Martyn Layzell
SURCD076

OPENING OUR HEARTS TO YOU

133

Highest Praise

James Gregory

(no capo)

Intro: A C#m7 F#m7 B7   D E A A

Verse 1:
```
            D                           E      F#m7
Opening our hearts to You, focusing our eyes on You
            D                           E      F#m7
Lifting up our hands to You, singing out this song for You
            D     Bm7              E      F#m7
Praises that will fill the skies, raising You over our lives
                E/G#
Lifting up the Saviour high
```

Chorus:
```
A                E/G#  F#m7  B7
We give You the highest praise
D              E       A    D : E
We give You the highest praise
A                E/G#  F#m7  B7
We give You the highest praise
D              E       A
We give You the highest praise
```

Verse 2:
You are so amazing Lord, a beautiful and mighty God
Compassionate and merciful, glorious and powerful
King over the universe, wonderfully in love with us
Passionate about the earth

Bridge:
```
      E          D
All glory, honour, worship, praise
      B7     B7/D#      E    C#7
With hands held high and voices raised
    F#m7  E     D          Esus  E
We offer up our hearts again to You
```

Taken from IS IT ANY WONDER
Heat
SURCD071

OPENING OUR HEARTS TO YOU

133

Highest Praise

James Gregory

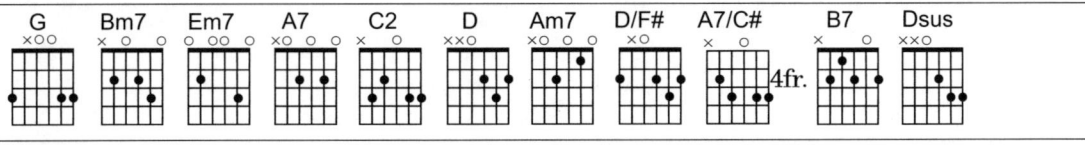

G   Bm7   Em7   A7   C2   D   Am7   D/F#   A7/C#   B7   Dsus

(Capo 2)

Intro: G   Bm7   Em7   A7   C2   D   G   G

Verse 1:
              C2   D   Em7
Opening our hearts to You, focusing our eyes on You
              C2   D   Em7
Lifting up our hands to You, singing out this song for You
                   C2   Am7   D   Em7
Praises that will fill the skies, raising You over our lives
                   D/F#
Lifting up the Saviour high

Chorus:
G   D/F#   Em7 A7
We give You the highest praise
C   D   G   C2 : D
We give You the highest praise
G   D/F#   Em7 A7
We give You the highest praise
C2   D   G
We give You the highest praise

Verse 2:
You are so amazing Lord, a beautiful and mighty God
Compassionate and merciful, glorious and powerful
King over the universe, wonderfully in love with us
Passionate about the earth

Bridge:
      D   C2
All glory, honour, worship, praise
     A7   A7/C#   D   B7
With hands held high and voices raised
    Em7 D   C2   Dsus   D
We offer up our hearts again to You

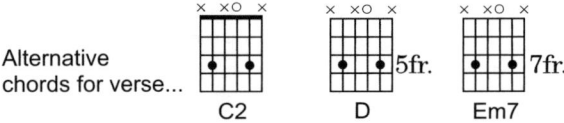

Alternative
chords for verse...

C2   D   Em7

Taken from IS IT ANY WONDER
Heat
SURCD071

OUR GOD IS BIG NOT SMALL

James Gregory

(no capo)

Intro: A E A C#5:D5   A E A C#5:D5   A E A C#5:D5   E

Verse 1:
```
          A       E       D A/C# E
Our God is big not small He loves us   all
D  E   A
He is amazing
          A       E       D C#m E
Our God is big not small He loves us    all
D  A/C#    E      D   A/C#    E      D   A/C#    Bm7
And we will praise Him  and we will praise Him  and we will praise
```

Chorus:
```
A        E/G#    A  A/C# D
What a wonderful God You are
A        E/G#    A  A/C# D
What a wonderful God You are
A        E/G#    A  A/C# D
What a wonderful God You are to us
```

Taken from IS IT ANY WONDER
Heat
SURCD071

OUR GOD IS BIG NOT SMALL

James Gregory

G	D	B5	C5	C2	G/B	Am7	D/F#

(Capo 2)

Intro: G D G B5:C5   G D G B5:C5   G D G B5:C5   D

Verse 1:
```
        G         D        C2 G/B D
Our God is big not small He loves  us  all
C2  D    G
He is amazing
        G         D        C2 G/B D
Our God is big not small He loves  us  all
C2  G/B       D      C2   G/B      D      C2   G/B        Am7
And we will praise Him  and we will praise Him  and we will praise
```


Chorus:
```
G        D/F#    G   G/B  C2
What a wonderful God You  are
G        D/F#    G   G/B  C2
What a wonderful God You  are
G        D/F#    G   G/B  C2
What a wonderful God You  are to us
```

Taken from IS IT ANY WONDER
Heat
SURCD071

Rise
Ken Riley

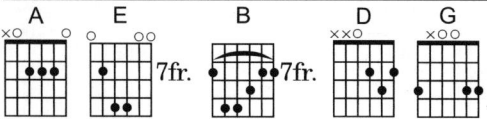

Verse 1:
A
Place the coal upon my lips
A
Deeds upon my fingertips
A   E
Actions whispering louder than my voice
A
Speak Your word out through the prophets
A
Make a sign bright like a comet
A   E
Jesus shining lighting up the sky

Chorus:
B   A   E
Rise and shine through us tonight

Verse 2:
Take me to the greatest need
A killer of the devils seed
Joining with the angels in Your song
Bind the hands of all abusers
Wipe the bullets from our future
C'mon God hear me dream out loud

Chorus 2:
B   A   E
Rise and shine though us Jesus
B   D
Rise and shine through us

Bridge:
E   D
Love, love is the drug I'm feeling
G   A
Love, love is the drug I'm dealing
E   D
Love, love what the world is needing
G   A   E
Rise, rise, tonight

Taken from
REVOLUTION
YFriday
SURCD093

PRAISE HIM YOU HEAVENS

Great In Power

Russell Fragar

D   G   G/D   Bm7   Asus4   A

Verse 1:
D
Praise Him you heavens and all that's above

Praise Him you angels and heavenly hosts
G   G/D   D
Let the whole earth praise Him
D
Praise Him the sun, moon and bright shining stars

Praise Him you heavens and waters and skies
G   G/D   D
Let the whole earth praise Him

Chorus:
D   Bm7
Great in power, great in glory
G   Bm7   Asus4 A
Great in mercy, King of hea - ven
D   Bm7
Great in battle, great in wonder
G   Bm7   Asus4 A   D
Great in Zion, King over all   the earth

Taken from
CHOSEN FROM THE NATIONS
Stoneleigh Live Worship 2000
KMCD2288

PRAISE THE LORD IN THE HEAVENS 137

Matt Redman

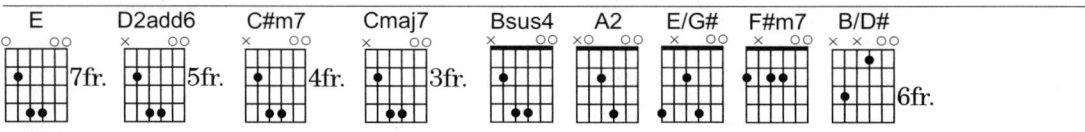

Verse 1:
E   D2add6
  Praise the Lord in the heavens
C#m7   Cmaj7
    Praise Him in the heights above
E   D2add6
  Praise Him all His angels
C#m7   Cmaj7
    Praise Him all His heavenly host
E   D2add6
  Praise Him sun and moon up high
C#m7   Cmaj7
    Praise Him all you stars that shine
Bsus4   A2
     Praise Him now you highest heavens
E/G#   F#m7
    All you waters above the skies

Chorus:
  E   F#m7
If we did not praise the rocks would cry out
  E/G#   A2
If we did not praise the rocks would cry out
  Bsus4   A2
If no song was sung in all of the earth
   B/D#   A2
The rocks would cry out Your praise

Verse 2:
Praise Him on the earth now
Creatures in the seas below
Lightning, hail and snow and clouds
Stormy winds that do His will
All you mountains, all you hills
All you creatures great and small
Kings and rulers of the earth
Come and praise Him young and old

Let Every Voice

Paul Oakley

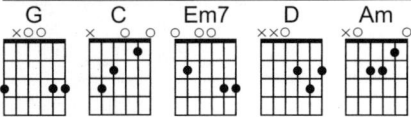

G   C   Em7   D   Am

(Capo 2)

Intro: A (G)   D (C)   F#m7 (Em7)   E (D)   x2

Verse 1:
A (G)   D (C)   E (D)
   Praises to the holy One
A (G)   D (C)   E (D)
   For the wonders You have done
F#m7 (Em7)   D (C)   E (D)
      Praise in every tribe and tongue
        Bm (Am)   E (D)
Jesus to You be sung

Verse 2:
Praise Him for His mighty power
Sun and moon and stars bow down
Praise in all creation now
Jesus to You resounds

Chorus:
A(G)   D (C)   F#m7 (Em7)
   Let every voice, let every song
      E (D)   A (G)
Let every instrument and sound
        D (C)   E (D)   D (C)
Declare the wonders of our God
A(G)   D (C)   F#m7 (Em7)   E (D)   A (G)
   Let all Your holy ones proclaim the glory of our Saviour's name
        D (C)   E (D)   D (C)
Let all the earth resound with praise, Jesus to You

Verse 3:
Angels help us to adore
As we bow our hearts in awe
Praise and honour evermore
Jesus to You our Lord

Bridge:
F#m7 (Em7)   D (C)   E (D)
      Let everything that lives and breathes
      D (C)   F#m7 (Em7)   D (C)   E (D)
Let every mountain, every sea reflect the beauty of our God
F#m7 (Em7)   D (C)   E (D)
      Let every heart burst into song
      D (C)   F#m7 (Em7)   D (C)   E (D)
Let every word upon my tongue declare the praise of who You are

Taken from
BE LIFTED UP
Paul Oakley
SURCD085

PRECIOUS

Vicky Beeching

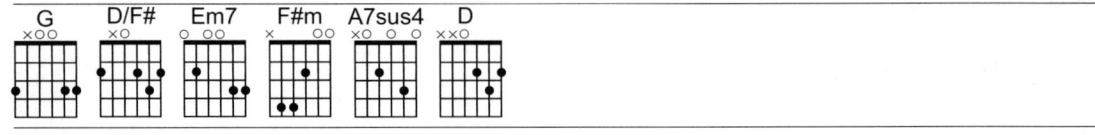

G   D/F#   Em7   F#m   A7sus4   D

Intro: G   D/F#   G   D/F#   x2

Verse 1:
G　　　　　D/F#
Precious are the moments
　　　G　　　　　D/F#
When I know that You are very near
G　　　　　D/F#
Precious are these moments
　　　Em7　　F#m
As You meet me here
　　　Em7　　G　　A7sus4
As You meet me here

Verse 2:
Treasured are the moments
When I know that You are very near
Treasured are these moments
As You meet me here
As You meet me here

Chorus:
D
Here with You
D/F#
Here with You
　　　G　　　　　Em7　　A7sus4
Your loving arms are holding me
D
Safe with You
D/F#
Safe with You
　　　G　　　　　A7sus4
There's nowhere else I'd rather be　　　(to intro)

Taken from SHELTER
Vicky Beeching
SURCD083

PUSHING ON

Greg Jong

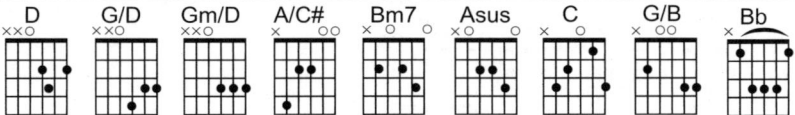

Intro: D G/D Gm/D D   x2

Verse 1:
D   G/D   Gm/D   D
Pushing on, on toward Your goal
D   G/D   Gm/D   D
Your goal for me
D   G/D   Gm/D   D
Christ Ahead, Spirit lead, I'm close
D   G/D   Gm/D   D
I'm close to You

Chorus:
D   A/C#   Bm7
And Your love will shine on
   Asus   C   G/B   Bb   Asus
Through the day, the night, in spite of all I do
D   A/C#   Bm7   Asus
And my hope, my strength, my shield
       C   G/B
Is found in You
            Bb   Asus   D
You've brought me into Your heart

Verse 2:
Born again, Jesus' friend
I know, I know You're here
Life to come with the One I love
I love You Lord

Taken from the
INTERNATIONAL PEOPLE'S ALBUM
Soul Survivor
SURCD054

Vicky Beeching

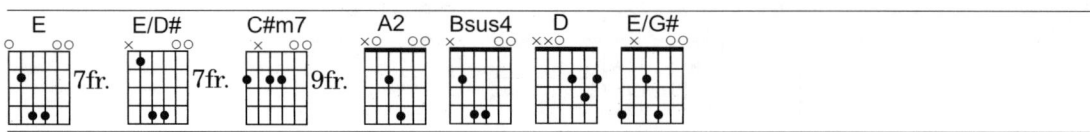

Verse:

E
Search me O God
         E/D#
Search me and find
C#m7   A   Bsus4
Any way in me that does not reflect Your purity
E
Refine me O Lord
         E/D#
In the fire of Your gaze
  C#m7   A   Bsus4
That I might be holy in all of my ways

Pre Chorus:

D   A   E
  Take me deeper Lord
D   A   E
  Draw me closer Lord

Chorus:

      E/G# A Bsus4
Give me a heart
           E/G# A Bsus4
That is after Your own heart
     C#m7   A   Bsus4
Give me a mind that is clean and pleasing unto You
        E/G# A Bsus4
Fill me up with Your love
     E/G# A   Bsus4
With Your power and Your joy
         D   A   E
That this world might see You in me
         D   A   E
That this world might see You in me

Taken from SHELTER
Vicky Beeching
SURCD083

Shepherd Of My Heart

Paul Oakley

| G | C | D | Em7 | D/F# |

(Capo 2)

Verse 1:
A (G)   D (C)   E (D)
Shepherd of my thankful heart
A (G)   D (C)   E (D)
Ever faithful friend You are
F#m7 (Em7)   D (C)   E (D)
Healer who now bears the scars
   F#m7 (Em7) E/G# (D/F#) D (C)
Of love's   amazing   grace

Verse 2:
Heaven's song made flesh for us
Crucified upon the cross
Now in glory Jesus
To You belongs all praise

Chorus:
   A (G)   D (C)   E (D)
Be glorified in me
    A (G)   D (C)   E (D)
Be glorified in me
  F#m7 (Em7) D (C)   E (D)
Be glorified   in   me
  F#m7 (Em7) E/G# (D/F#) D (C)
Jesus,   my King

Verse 3:
Sacrifice no words could tell
Majesty on earth to dwell
Living Word, Emmanuel
I'll love You all my days

Verse 4:
Maker of the stars above
Praise of angels ever sung
King of glory, King of love
Let all creation praise
Let all creation praise
Let all creation praise

Taken from
BE LIFTED UP
Paul Oakley
SURCD085

SING ME WITH A SONG OF LOVE

Songs Of Heaven

Ken Riley

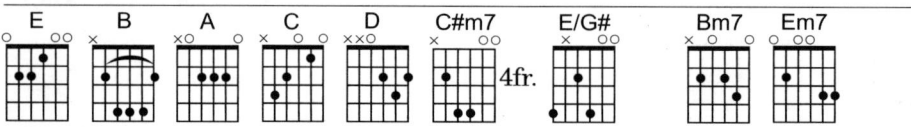

Verse 1:
E (F#)   B (C#)
Sing me with a song of love
A (B)   B (C#)
Pouring out from heaven above
E (F#)   B (C#)   A (B)   B (C#)
Clothe me with a melody of praise
E (F#)   B (C#)
Hear my invitation come
A (B)   B (C#)
Let Your Spirit over run
E (F#)   B (C#)   A (B)   B (C#)
All I am and all I hope to be
    C (D)   D (E)
A reflection of my King

Chorus:
E (F#)   B (C#)
Singing songs of heaven and
    C#m7 (D#m7)   A (B)
I am singing songs of love
E/G# (F#/A#)   B (C#)   A (B)   B (C#)
Joining heaven's anthem to my God above
E (F#)   B (C#)
Singing songs of heaven
C#m7 (D#m7)   A (B)
I am shouting out Your name
E/G# (F#/A#)   B (C#)   A (B)   B (C#)
Joining heaven's angels in Your song of praise

Verse 2:
Let the passion of Your song, touch my spirit, lead me on
Reaching out to seek and save the lost
Flood the world with heaven's saints, radical for Jesus name
Gathering our harvest of the free
Now abandoned to my King

Tag:
      E (F#) B (C#)   A (B)   B (C#)
Sing Your pra - ise, sing Your praise
      E (F#) B (C#)   A (B)   B (C#)
Sing Your pra - ise, sing Your praise

Taken from
SONGS OF HEAVEN
YFriday
YFCD02

Sing To The Lord   **Andy Ferrett & Marc James**

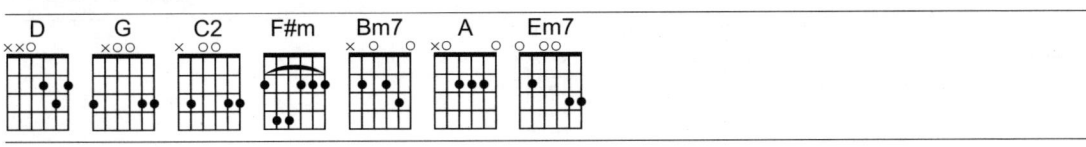

Verse 1:

D   G   D
  Sing to the Lord for He is good
               G
Give thanks to Him
D   G   C2
  Tell all the world of all He's done
D   G   D
  Come lift Your voice to worship Him
            G
Come shout aloud
F#m   G   Bm7
    Open up you gates, you ancient doors
         A
Let His glory in

Chorus:

D   G
Hallelujah, King forever
Bm7   A   G
All the earth will bow
D   G
God most holy, You're so worthy
Bm7   A   G
We will praise You now

Verse 2:

He is a God of favour, mercy and grace
He reaches out with arms held wide
Who is this King of glory?
He's Lord of all
Open up you gates, you ancient doors
Let His glory in

Bridge:

Em7   G   Em7   G
    Let the heavens rejoice,   let the earth be glad
Em7   G   A
    Let the seas resound with praise
Em7   G   Em7   G
    Let us join as one,   with creation's song
Em7   G   C2
    Lifting up a sound of praise

Taken from
BE LIFTED UP
Paul Oakley
SURCD085

SON OF GOD

The Greatest Gift

145

Vicky Beeching

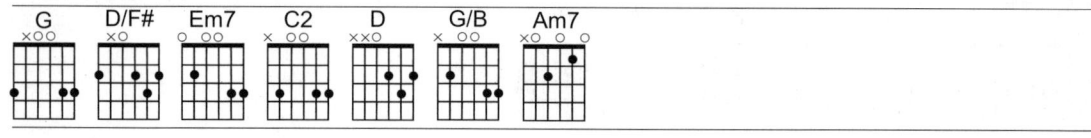

Capo 3

Verse 1:
```
G        D/F#  Em7           C2
Son of God        You reign in heaven's glory
G        D/F#  Em7           C2
Yet You chose      to come to earth and save me
Em7                        C2
     Humbled Yourself to die the cruelest death
Em7                       C2          D
     No other act of love compares to this
```

Chorus:
```
              G            G/B
The greatest gift I've ever received
        C2        D
Is the cross, the cross
              G            G/B
For there You gave Yourself up for me
        C2        D
On the cross, the cross
              Em7            G/B
And with the blood You poured out for me
        C2        D
You have saved my soul
Am7      G/B  C2     D            G  G/B  C2  D  (or to Middle Eight)
You have given me the greatest gift of all
```

Verse 2:
Your heart aches for all the lost and hurting
At the cross You wait to take our burdens
Longing to heal our wounds and make us whole
Longing to hear us sing with thankful souls

Middle Eight:
```
Am7  G/B  C2  D
Am7  G/B  C2  D  D
```

Taken from SHELTER
Vicky Beeching
SURCD083

Verse 1:
Bb   F/A Gm7   Eb
Son of God   You reign in heaven's glory
Bb   F/A Gm7   Eb
Yet You chose   to come to earth and save me
Gm7   Eb
     Humbled Yourself to die the cruelest death
Gm7   Eb   F
     No other act of love compares to this

Chorus:
             Bb   Bb/D
The greatest gift I've ever received
      Eb   F
Is the cross, the cross
            Bb   Bb/D
For there You gave Yourself up for me
       Eb   F
On the cross, the cross
          Gm7   Bb/D
And with the blood You poured out for me
        Eb   F
You have saved my soul
Cm7   Bb/D Eb   F   Bb Bb/D Eb F (or to Middle Eight)
You have given me the greatest gift of all

Verse 2:
Your heart aches for all the lost and hurting
At the cross You wait to take our burdens
Longing to heal our wounds and make us whole
Longing to hear us sing with thankful souls

Middle Eight:
Cm7 Bb/D Eb F
Cm7 Bb/D Eb F F

Taken from SHELTER
Vicky Beeching
SURCD083

SON OF GOD

Hallelujah

Marc James

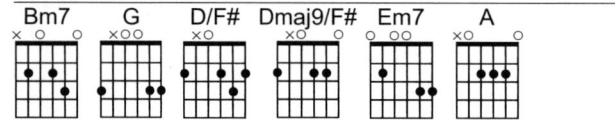

Intro: Bm7   G   D/F#   G   (x2)

Verse 1:
Bm7   G   D/F#   G
   Son of God You came to save us from darkness
Bm7   G   D/F#   G
   Came to break the chains that bind and enslave us
Bm7   G   D/F#   G
   As You walked You showed us mercy and kindness
Bm7   G   D/F#   G
   And You taught us how to pray so we're praying

Pre-Chorus:
     Dmaj9/F#   G
That Your kingdom come
     Dmaj9/F#   G
That Your will be done
    Dmaj9/F# G   Em7   D/F#   G
On the earth as it is in heaven

Chorus:
   A   D/F#   G
Hallelujah
      A   D/F#   G
Come and reign
   A   D/F#   G
Hallelujah
       A   D/F#   G
We're praying again

Verse 2:
When the Spirit comes as power and healing
And everyone can know salvation and meaning
And the blind can see the dead arising
Where Your people start to pray we're praying

Taken from
ON THE STREETS
Festival Manchester
SURCD095

SOVEREIGN LORD

Majesty

Martyn Layzell

Verse 1:
G Em7
Sovereign Lord, over all
C2 G D/F#
You are reigning forever
G Em7
Glory flows, from Your lips
C2 G D/F#
We have come for just one glimpse

Pre-Chorus:
C2 D Em7 D/F#
And we sing a - lle - lu - ia
C2 D Em7 D/F#
A - lle - lu - ia
C2 D Em7 A7 C
A - lle - lu - ia

Chorus:
G Em7
Majesty, reign in me
D/F# C2
Your right hand enfolding me
G Em7
Earth applaud, heavens sing
D/F# C2
At the sight of Christ the King

Verse 2:
Lord of Lords, now enthroned
Who can stand in Your presence?
Fire of love, holy One
You burn brighter than the sun

Taken from LOST IN WONDER
Martyn Layzell
SURCD076

STANDING ON HOLY GROUND

Holy Ground

Paul Oakley & Martin Cooper

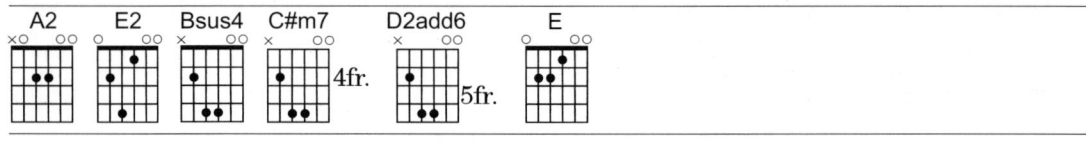

Verse 1:

      A2   E2
Standing on holy ground
      Bsus4   C#m7
Mercy and grace I've found
D2add6
     I'm here before Your throne now
A2   Bsus4
  By a new and living way

Verse 2:
Jesus I come to You
I lift up my eyes to You
How You've comforted me
And now I long to see Your face

Chorus:

      A2   E
You are my strength, my song
      A2   E
You are my shield, my redeemer
      A2   E   Bsus4
You are my hope, my salvation, and my God
  A2   E   Bsus4   A2 E2 A2 E2
I'll always bring my praise to You O God

Chorus 2:

      A2   E
You are my strength, my song
      A2   E
You are my shield, my redeemer
      A2   E   Bsus4
You are my hope, my salvation, and my God
    A2   E   A2   E
So I will sing to You, beautiful things You have done
       A2   E   Bsus4
Great is Your name in Zion, holy One
  A2   E   Bsus4
I'll always bring my praise to You
  A2   E   Bsus4
I'll always bring my praise to You
  A2   E   Bsus4   A2 E2 A2 E2
I'll always bring my praise to You, O God

Taken from
BE LIFTED UP
Paul Oakley
SURCD085

THERE IS A DAY

Nathan Fellingham

C2   Cmaj7   Am   F   C/E   G   Gsus4   C   Fmaj7

Verse 1:
```
C2            Cmaj7              Am
   There is a day   that all creation's waiting for
F             C/E                    G
 A day of freedom   and liberation for the earth
C2              Cmaj7                Am
   And on that day   the Lord will come to meet His bride
F                 C/E               Gsus4    G
 And when we see Him   in an instant we'll be changed
```

Verse 2:
The trumpet sounds and the dead will then be raised
By His power, never to perish again
Once only flesh, now clothed with immortality
Death has now been swallowed up in victory

Chorus:
```
C                        G
  We will meet Him in the air
                    Am
And then we will be like Him
            F         C    G
For we will see Him as He is, oh yeah!
C                        G
  Then all hurt and pain will cease
                      Am
And we'll be with Him forever
          F         C
And in His glory we will live
      G      Fmaj7
Oh yeah, oh yeah!
```

Verse 3:
So lift your eyes to the things as yet unseen
That will remain now for all eternity
Though trouble's hard, it's only momentary
And it's achieving our future glory

Taken from HOPE
Phatfish Unplugged
FOCD004

THERE IS A GREAT SALVATION

150

Nathan & Luke Fellingham

Call

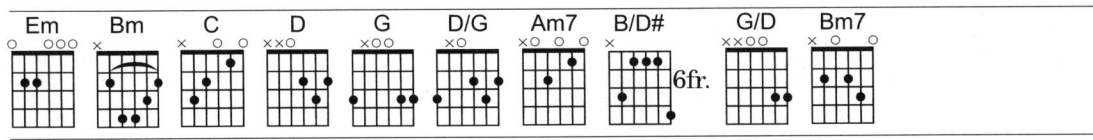

Verse 1:
```
Em                      Bm   C                        Em
    There is a great salvation  to be made known to every nation
     D         C        D
That Jesus will return
Em                      Bm        C                        Em
    And we have been commissioned,  we're called to go and make disciples
     D            C
Baptising all who follow
```

Pre-Chorus:
```
          D   G    D/G     Am7                  G
And all authority is given to the Son, reigning over all
       D/G    Am7              Em
Death He has destroyed, the church rises strong
       Bm      C      D
The battle has been won
```

Chorus:
```
Em                  B/D#                  G/D
    We will take hold of the call to go and make the gospel known
              Am7           Bm7          Em
To all the world, teaching all the goodness of the Lord
              B/D#                    G/D
Father let Your kingdom come and Holy Spirit burn in us and let our lives
   Am7       Bm7           Em
Be worthy of the call we have received
```

Verse 2:
```
There is a pure religion to clothe the poor and feed the hungry
With mercy handed forth
With acts of selfless giving rooted in love and compassion
We'll show the love of Jesus
```

Taken from
ON THE STREETS
Festival Manchester 2003
SURCD095

THERE'S A PAGEANT OF TRIUMPH 151

David Fellingham

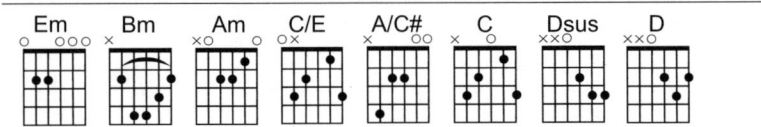

(Capo 3)

Intro: Gm (Em)   Dm (Bm)   Cm (Am)   Dm (Bm)   x4

Verse 1:
         Gm (Em)   Dm (Bm) Cm (Am) Dm (Bm)
There's a pageant of triumph in glo - ry
     Gm (Em)   Dm (Bm)   Cm (Am) Dm (Bm)
As Jesus the King takes His throne
         Gm (Em)   Dm (Bm) Cm (Am)   Dm (Bm)
The shame of the cross is exchanged for a crown
         Gm (Em)   Dm (Bm)   Cm (Am)
And heaven   applauds the King
         Gm (Em)   Dm (Bm) Cm (Am) Dm (Bm)
The Son has the Father's   approval
     Gm (Em)   Dm (Bm)   Cm (Am)   Dm (Bm)
He perfectly followed the plan
     Gm (Em)   Dm (Bm)   Cm (Am)   Dm (Bm)
To suffer and die for the sins of the world
     Gm (Em)   Dm (Bm)   Cm (Am)   Dm (Bm)
He poured out His love for our shame

Chorus:
Gm (Em)   C/E (A/C#)   Eb (C)
   Let God arise with shouts of joy
                   Fsus (Dsus)   Gm (Em)
With songs of praise and trumpet sound
                   C/E (A/C#)   Eb (C)
Let music play and hearts be free
       F (D) Gm (Em)
Let God   arise   (rpt)

Verse 2:
Death could not keep Him in prison
He burst through the shackles of hell
He's settled the score with the evil one
And heaven applauds the King
The fullness of Christ is my treasure
I've cast off the past with its shame
The power of the Father has raised me to life
I'm a son, I'm forgiven , I'm free

Taken from DREAMS & VISIONS
Re:vive@Stoneleigh
SURCD059

THERE MUST BE MORE

Consuming Fire

Tim Hughes

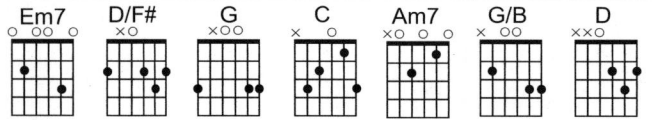

Em7 D/F# G C Am7 G/B D

Verse 1:
```
 Em7          D/F#      G
There must be more than this
C           Em7      D/F#    C
O breath of God come breathe within
 Em7         D/F#      G
There must be more than this
  C     Em7   D/F#    C
Spirit of God we wait for You
Am7   G/B       D
Fill us anew we pray
Am7   G/B       D
Fill us anew we pray
```

Chorus:
```
            G           D/F#
Consuming fire, fan into flame
    Em7           C
A passion for Your name
          G           D/F#
Spirit of God fall in this place
                Em7
Lord have Your way
                D/F#      C
Lord have Your way with us
```

Verse 2:
Come like a rushing wind
Clothe us with power from on high
Now set the captives free
Leave us abandoned to Your praise
Lord let Your glory fall
Lord let Your glory fall

God Of Great Things   Johnny Parks

(no capo)

Verse 1:
```
          B      E    B    E
There's a new song upon my lips
   B    E    B    E
A song I always knew
B    Bsus   A  Amaj7    B  E B  E
Thank You for all that You do
           B        E      B   E
There is a fire burning in my heart
   B     E    B    E
A fire of faith in You
    B    Bsus   A   Amaj7   B  E  B   E
I believe all the things we can do
```

Pre-Chorus:
```
G#7              C#m7
You're the God of great things
G#7              C#m7
You're the God of great things
  B6    Amaj7               B6
I won't hold back my thanks to You
```

Chorus:
```
E           B         A        B
Thank You, Thank You, hey Jesus I adore You
E           B         A        B
Thank You, Thank You, hey Jesus I live for You
```

Verse 2:
There is a beat pounding through my feet
A new dance of thanks to You
I'm tasting the joy found in You
There is courage building in my heart
A strength that comes from You
I'm going to live life for You

Taken from CLOSE TO YOU
Johnny Parks
SURCD055

THERE'S A NEW SONG

God Of Great Things

Johnny Parks

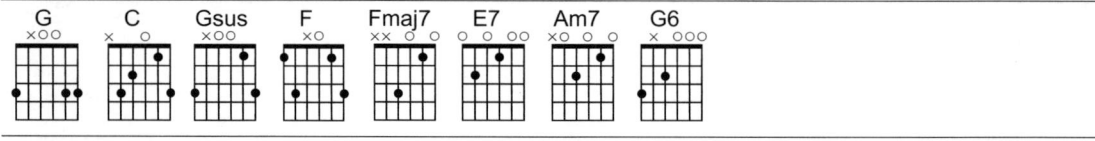

(Capo 4)

Verse 1:
```
        G        C       G   C
There's a new song upon my lips
  G    C      G   C
A song I always knew
  G   Gsus  F Fmaj7   G C G  C
Thank You for all that You do
          G        C      G   C
There is a fire burning in my heart
  G    C      G    C
A fire of faith in You
   G   Gsus    F   Fmaj7   G C G  C
I believe all the things we can do
```

Pre-Chorus:
```
E7               Am7
You're the God of great things
E7               Am7
You're the God of great things
  G6  Fmaj7                G6
I won't hold back my thanks to You
```

Chorus:
```
C          G        F     G
Thank You, Thank You, hey Jesus I adore You
C          G        F     G
Thank You, Thank You, hey Jesus I live for You
```

Verse 2:
There is a beat pounding through my feet
A new dance of thanks to You
I'm tasting the joy found in You
There is courage building in my heart
A strength that comes from You
I'm going to live life for You

Taken from CLOSE TO YOU
Johnny Parks
SURCD055

THIS IS HOW I KNOW WHAT LOVE IS

154

David Gate

Extravagant

D   A7sus4   G/B   Bm7   G

Verse 1:
```
D           A7sus4    G/B  D
This is how I know what love is
D           A7sus4    G/B  D
This is how I know what love is
D              A7sus4 G/B  Bm7
Jesus took the cross in mer - cy
   G    A7sus4  D
A love I don't deserve
```

Chorus:
```
   G           Bm7
Extravagant, magnificent
      G            D
The love You pour on me
   G           Bm7
Extravagant, magnificent
     G            A7sus4
Your grace I have received
```

Verse 2:
```
   D            A7sus4  G/B    D
Now everything I am must praise You
D          A7sus4  G/B    D
Everything I am must praise You
      D           A7sus4 G/B  D
And everything I have I  give You
   G      A7sus4 D
A life You so   deserve
```

TO YOU KING JESUS

Nathan Fellingham

Chords: E5 Cmaj7 D Am Em D/F# G Gmaj7 C G/B

Intro: E5   Cmaj7   D   E5   Cmaj7   D

Verse 1:
E5   Cmaj7   D
   To You King Jesus we sing our song
E5   Cmaj7 D
   The first and the last, the living One
Am   Em   D/F#
   With eyes like fire and feet like bronze
                      G   Am
Your face shines brighter than the sun
        Em   D
All creation speaks Your name

Chorus:
G Gmaj7   Em   C   Em
Je - sus, Son of God, You stand in all authority
                    D
And at Your name darkness flees
   G Gmaj7   Em   C   G/B
Oh Je - sus living Word, reigning at the Father's right hand
          Em   C   Am G/B D
And You're clothed with majesty and po - wer

Verse 2:
To You King Jesus we bring our hearts
For You have come to us with Your great love
You suffered death, went to the grave
But now You're crowned with glory
All Your people speak Your name

Bridge:
C   Em   C
   And we now stand at Your side, a people chosen as Your bride
                          Em   D/F# G   C
You've filled us with the Spirit's power, this is   the hour
                          Em   C
So in Your strength I'll run this race, covered by Your daily grace
              G/B   C
Pressing on towards the prize, til the day that You return
              G/B   D
And every tribe and every tongue will sing:

Taken from
GLIMPSES OF GLORY
Soul Survivor Live 2002
SURCD082

TO YOUR CROSS I COME AGAIN

Close To Me

Trè Sheppard

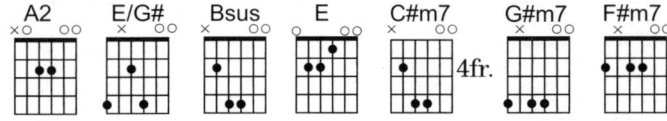

A2 E/G# Bsus E C#m7 G#m7 F#m7

Intro: A2 E/G# Bsus A2 E/G# Bsus x2

Verse 1:
E
To Your cross I come again
E
Open heart with all I am
E
At Your feet I come and bow
E
Eternal God be near me now

Chorus:
C#m7 Bsus A2   G#m7
     All I want is You here
C#m7 Bsus A2   G#m7
     All I need is You near
C#m7 Bsus A2   G#m7
     All I want is You here
F#m7 Bsus   F#m7   Bsus
Close to me, come close to me
A2 E/G# Bsus   A2 E/G# Bsus   A2 E/G# Bsus
Je - sus, Je - sus, Je - sus
    F#m7   Bsus   F#m7   Bsus
Come close to me, come close to me

Verse 2:
Creator of all time and space
You chose the cross and this is grace
A love like this who could repay
So here with You Lord I will stay

Extra Chorus:
 A2   E   Bsus A2   E   Bsus
I want You here with me, I need You here with me
 A2   E   Bsus A2   E   Bsus
I want You here with me, I feel You close to me

Taken from CARDIPHONIA
100 Hours
SURCD073

TROUBLES FLOW AS WATERFALLS

Lament

Ken Riley

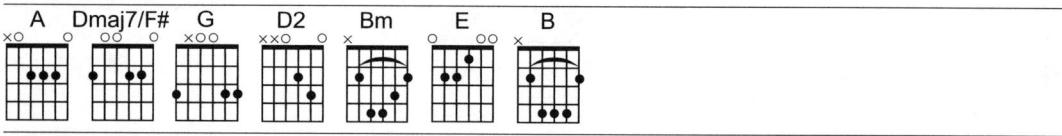

Verse 1:
A   Dmaj7/F#
Troubles flow as waterfalls
G   D2
Waves of sorrow crush me
A   Dmaj7/F#
Tears that flood a thousand streams
      G   D2
My heart a million pieces

Pre-Chorus:
Bm
     There's a hole inside
A
   There's a hole inside
Bm   E
     There's a hole inside my soul

Verse 2:
Joy becomes a faded dream
Peace a distant echo
Hope am I abandoned here?
Faith I feel you shaking

Instrumental Section:
B E D E
B E D E

Verse 3:
A   Dmaj7/F# G   D
Night explodes in symphony, breaking through my shadows
A   Dmaj7/F# G   D
Fighting my uncertainty, I step out on the water

Tag:
A   Dmaj7/F#   G   D
Lord, will You stretch Your hand out, Your hand out
A   Dmaj7/F#   G   D
Lord, will You stretch Your hand out, Your hand out

Verse 4:
More than all the world can give
I am thirsting for You

Taken from
REVOLUTION
YFriday
SURCD093

WALKING ROUND THESE CITY WALLS 158

My Little Jerichos

Paul Oakley

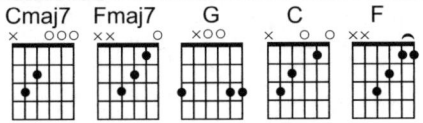

Cmaj7 Fmaj7 G C F

Cmaj7   Fmaj7   Cmaj7
   Ba dap bup bup bah, a dap bup bup bah
              Fmaj7   Cmaj7
Ba dap bup bup bah, a dap bup bup bah

Verse 1:
Cmaj7   Fmaj7
   Walking round these city walls, seeing objects in my way
Cmaj7   Fmaj7
   Am I blind or just a fool? Did I hear the words You said?
Cmaj7   Fmaj7
   Trust my heart above my eyes, to believe and never doubt
Cmaj7   Fmaj7   Cmaj7   Fmaj7
   And these walls I'm staring at, will all come tumbling down yeah

Verse 2: (as verse 1)
Surely I can find the faith, or at least a mustard seed
For You've placed it in my heart, on the day I first believed
          Fmaj7   G
So if I can invest it   in the One who made all things

Chorus:
C   F
  I can walk on water, I can move a mountain
C   F   G
  I can rise above it, I can fly on eagles' wings
      C   F   G
And I know the One I've trusted to be faithful

Verse 3:
So I face the day ahead, with a fire inside of me
Moving in the strength I have, knowing You are with me
            Fmaj7   G
And I'll cling to the promises   of the One who made all things

Chorus 2:
C   F
You bring water from a rock, make a pathway through the sea
C   F   G
You breathe life into the dead, and You made this blind man see
     C   F   G
And I know the One I've trusted to be faithful
     C   F   G
And there's nothing in this world too hard for Him
Cmaj7   Fmaj7
Ba bap bup bup bah, Ba bap bup bup bah...

Taken from UNAFRAID
Paul Oakley
SURCD081

WE ARE THOSE

Adam's Race

Paul Oakley

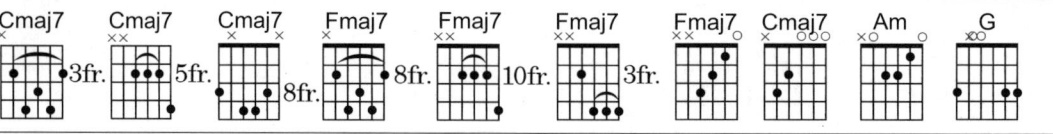

[Chorus   ]

Verse 1:
Cmaj7
We are those whom You have made
                          Fmaj7
Fashioned in the image of our God
      Cmaj7
But Adam sinned and disobeyed
                         Fmaj7
Now we face the consequences and the loss
Cmaj7
I have never seen Your face
                              Fmaj7
Or heard Your footsteps near me but I   have to say
Cmaj7
Had it been me I'd have done the same
                          Fmaj7
Something in me always wants my way

Chorus:
             Fmaj7   Cmaj7
But You're changing me by Your power within
      Fmaj7   Am   G
And I could sing of all Your grace
            Fmaj7   Cmaj7
And You're making me to be like him
      Fmaj7   Cmaj7 G
Who bled and died for Adam's race

Verse 2:
We are weak, but You are strong
We are foolish, but You are so wise
We are helpless, but You help us
We are just like children in Your eyes
We are selfish, but You're selfless
We are impure, but You are so pure
We're imperfect but You're perfect
We are broken, but You are so whole

Taken from UNAFRAID
Paul Oakley
SURCD081

WE CALL UPON YOUR NAME 160

Arise King Of Kings Mick Goss, Becky Heaslip & Eoghan Heaslip

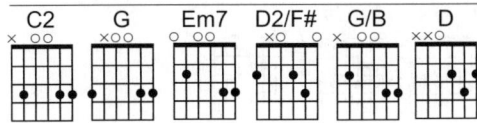

C2 G Em7 D2/F# G/B D

Verse:
Db2 (C2)
We call upon Your name O Lord
Ab (G)
  The name that is holy
Db2 (C2)
We call upon Your name O Lord
Ab (G)
  The name that is holy   (repeat)

Pre-Chorus:
Fm7 (Em7)   Db2 (C2)
We call upon Your Name O Lord
Ab (G)   Eb2/G (D2/F#)
We come to bring our praise to the One
     Fm7 (Em7) Db2 (C2)
Who was,   who is
   Ab/C (G/B) Eb (D)
And is   to   come

Chorus:
  Ab (G)   Eb2/G (D2/F#)
Arise King of kings
Eb (D)   Fm7 (Em7)   Db2 (C2) Eb(D)
God of all creation, O Lord we cry
  Ab (G)   Eb2/G (D2/F#)
Arise King of kings
     Eb (D)   Fm7 (Em7)
The Father to the nations
     Eb2/G (D2/F#)   Db2 (C2) Eb (D)
The Rock of our salvation
        Db2 (C2)   Ab (G)   Db2 (C2)   Ab (G)
O God arise

Taken from
MERCY
Eoghan Heaslip
Hosanna 22482

WE COME TO YOUR MOUNTAIN

Call To Worship

Matt Redman

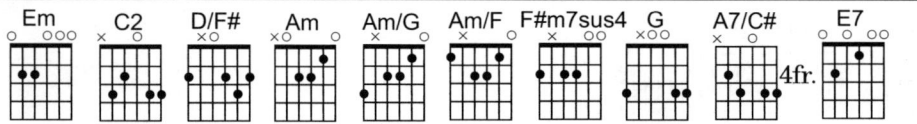

Verse 1:
Em   C2
We come to Your mountain
Em   C2   D/F#   Em
The hill of the Lord we would ascend
                 C2   D/F# Em
And journey into your holy place

Verse 2:
Em   C2
To feast in Your presence
Em   C2   D/F#   Em
And bring our devotions to You God
                C2   D/F#   Em
We come as a kingdom of Your priests

Chorus A:
                          Am
We're climbing up the mountain of the Lord
 Am/G   Am/F
Towards Your holy place, and every step is praise
 Am/G   Am
Encountering the glory of Your name
   Am/G   F#m7sus4
Your throne of holiness, the wonders of Your grace

Chorus B:
  Em   G
O come, come let us worship
       A7/C#   C2   D/F#   Em
Come let us recognize what a sacred thing we do
      G
Come let us bow down
      A7/C#   C2   D/F#   Em   (E7 into Inst. Section)
God as we bring our hearts let them please the heart of You

Verse 3:
We enter Your sanctuary to minister at Your holy throne
Where thousands of angels joyfully sing

Taken from
WHERE ANGELS FEAR TO TREAD
Matt Redman
SURCD074

WE COULD WATCH YOU FROM AFAR   162

Rejoice With Trembling

Matt Redman

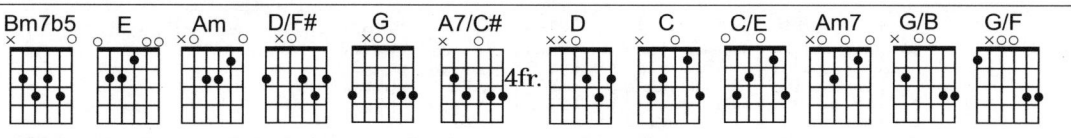

Intro: Bm7b5   E   Am   D/F#   x2

Verse 1:
Bm7b5   E   Am
We could watch You from afar
        D/F#   G
And forever be amazed
            A7/C#   D
At how glorious You are
Bm7b5   E   Am
Yet You've drawn us close to You
              D/F#   G
Where the wonder's greater still
            A7/C#   D   C
And You overwhelm us God

Chorus:
              G   D/F#   Bm7b5
And we rejoice with trembling in our hearts
        C/E   Am7   G/B   C
Bring You a song of reverence and love
        G   D/F#   Bm7b5
Jesus how good how great You are
          C   Am7   G/B C   G
And we rejoice with trembling   before Your throne

Verse 2:
Bm7b5   E   Am
Who could fully voice the praise
        D/F#   G
Of the God of endless days
        A7/C#   D
Tell a fraction of Your worth
Bm7b5   E   Am
For we only sing in part
        D/F#   G
Of the grace of who You are
        A7/C#   D   C
Just an echo just a glimpse

Inst Section:
G   D/F#   G/F   C

Taken from
WHERE ANGELS FEAR TO TREAD
Matt Redman
SURCD074

Lord Of The Harvest

Matt Redman

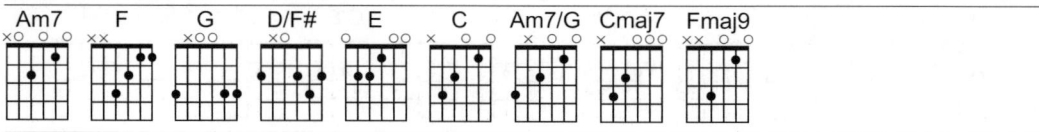

Am7   F   G   D/F#   E   C   Am7/G   Cmaj7   Fmaj9

Verse 1:
```
        Am7    F    G
We journey on
                  Am7    F    G
To see the kingdom come
            Am7    F    G
With eyes of faith
            Am7    F    G
Fixed on You alone
```

Pre-Chorus:
```
Am7          G           D/F#
    And if we go and sow in tears
        G              Am7
We will return with songs of joy
        G              D/F#
And Lord in faith we'll persevere
        G              E
Until we see the harvest come
```

Chorus:
```
          C                 F
You're the Lord, Lord of the harvest
      Am7          Am7/G        D/F#    E
We're singing out and shouting out Your fame
          C                 F
You're the Lord, Lord of the harvest
      Am7          Am7/G        D/F#    E
You send us in the power of Your name
              Am7
Lord of the harvest
```

Verse 2:
So let Your truth
Be song throughout the earth
Your gospel spread
Through wonders, works and words

Bridge:
```
Cmaj7              Fmaj9   D/F#                E
    This will be our worship,    this will be our worship
Cmaj7              Fmaj9   D/F#                E
    This will be our worship,    this will be our worship
```

Taken from
ON THE STREETS
Festival Manchester 2003
SURCD095

WE STAND UPON YOUR HOLINESS

164

Come In Power

Ken Riley

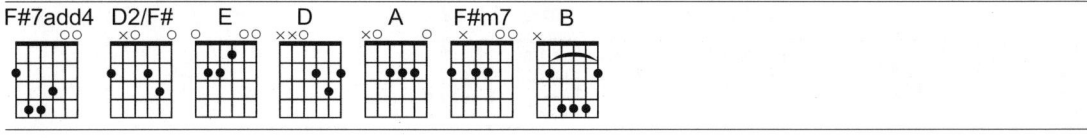

F#7add4   D2/F#   E   D   A   F#m7   B

Verse 1:
F#7add4
      We stand upon Your holiness
D2/F#
    We stand upon Your blood
F#7add4
      We cry out for the prodigals
D2/F#
    The souls of the lost
  E   **D**
O Lord come and release Your baptism of fire

Chorus:
 A   **D**   **F#m7**   **E**
Jesus, Jesus, come in power, come in power
 A   **D**   **F#m7**   **B**
Jesus, Jesus, come in power, come in power
D   **E**
   We cry to You

Verse 2:
With sounds of guitars and drums
And voices shouting out
We're weapons of the Holy One taking ground
O Lord come and release Your baptism of fire

Taken from
SONGS OF HEAVEN
YFriday
YFCD02

Facedown

Matt Redman

Am   E   Cmaj7   D2   Fmaj9   C   Am/G   Fmaj9/G

(Capo 6)

Verse 1:
Am   E
     Welcomed in to the courts of the King
      Cmaj7   **D2**
I've been ushered in to Your presence
Am   **E**
     Lord I stand on Your merciful ground
      Cmaj7   **D2**
Yet with every step tread with reverence

Verse 2:
There is none in the heavens like You
And upon the earth, who's Your equal?
You are far above, You're the highest of heights
  Cmaj7   **Fmaj9**
I am bowing down to exalt You

Chorus:
        C   **Fmaj9**
And I'll fall facedown
       Am   Am/G   **Fmaj9**
As Your glory shines around
       C   **Fmaj9**
Yes, I'll fall facedown
       Am   Am/G   **Fmaj9**   **D2   Fmaj9**
As Your glory shines around

Tag:
Fmaj9   **Fmaj9/G**
     Let Your glory shine around
             Fmaj9
Let Your glory shine around
             Fmaj9/G
King of glory, here be found

King of glory

Facedown
Matt Redman

Verse 1:
Ebm   Bb
    Welcomed in to the courts of the King
     Gbmaj7   Ab2
I've been ushered in to Your presence
Ebm   Bb
     Lord I stand on Your merciful ground
     Gbmaj7   Ab2
Yet with every step tread with reverence

Verse 2:
There is none in the heavens like You
And upon the earth, who's Your equal?
You are far above, You're the highest of heights
  Gbmaj7   Bmaj9
I am bowing down to exalt You

Chorus:
      Gb   Bmaj9
And I'll fall facedown
       Ebm Ebm/Db Bmaj9
As Your glory shines around
      Gb   Bmaj9
Yes, I'll fall facedown
       Ebm Ebm/Db Bmaj9   Ab2   Bmaj9
As Your glory shines around

Tag:
Bmaj9   Bmaj9/Db
    Let Your glory shine around
          Bmaj9
Let Your glory shine around
           Bmaj9/Db
King of glory, here be found

King of glory

WERE THERE WORDS

Trè Sheppard

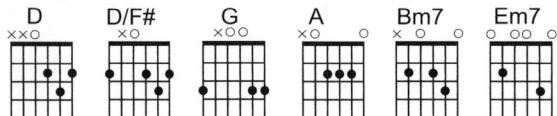

```
 D      D/F#     G       A      Bm7     Em7
xx o    x o     x oo    x o  o  x o  o   o oo o
```

Intro: D D/F# G A x2

Verse 1:
```
D                 D/F#      G        A
```
Were there words enough to praise You
```
D                 D/F#     G        A
```
Were there songs enough to sing
```
Bm7            D/F#        G                              A
```
Were there ways enough to thank You for the things You've done
```
D                 D/F#     G        A
```
Then I would give You everything

Verse 2:
If only every heart would lift You
If only every voice would sing
If only all the earth would raise a holy hallelujah
From everyone and everything

Chorus:
```
        D    D/F# G   A         D  D/F#  G  A
```
Strong deliverer,   friend and king
```
    Bm7  D/F# G          A         D  D/F#  G  A
```
Abba Father,   let the whole world sing
```
        D    D/F# G            A         D  D/F#  G  A
```
Of Your holiness   and Your unending love
```
    Bm7           G        A     D    G  A
```
I will lift my life to You, I will lift You up

Verse 3:
There will be words enough to praise You
There will be words enough to sing
There will be ways enough to thank You for the things You've done
And we will give You everything

Verse 4:
For one day every heart will lift You
One day every voice will sing
One day from the streets we'll hear the sound of a hallelujah
From everyone and everything

Bridge:
```
Em7 D/F# G       Em7 D/F# G          Em7 D/F# G
```
         With all I am   and all I'm not
```
    Em7                 D/F#                       G
```
With all I am and all I'm not I have come to lift You up
```
    Em7                 D/F#                       G
```
With all I am and all I'm not I have come to lift You up
```
    Em7                 D/F#                       G
```
With all I am and all I'm not I have come to lift You up

Taken from CARDIPHONIA
100 Hours
SURCD073

WHEN I AM LOST

I Have Been Redeemed

Wendy O'Connell

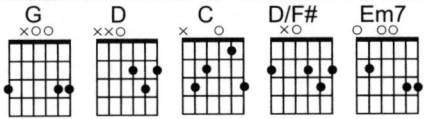

(Capo4)

Verse 1:
B (G)   F# (D)   B (G)
 When I am   lost
       E (C)   F# (D)
When I am all alone
   B (G)
Burdened by my sin and shame
            E (C)   F# (D)   B (G)
There 's one place I can go

Pre-Chorus:
   E (C)   F# (D)
I look towards the Cross
   B (G)   F#/A# (D/F#)   G#m7 (Em7)
Where my Saviour   died
   E (C)   F# (D)
Suffered in my place
       B (G)   F#/A# (D/F#) G#m7 (Em7)
The perfect sacri   -   fice
       E (C)   F# (D)
For me so I can know

Chorus:
   B (G) F# (D)   E (C)
Now I am forgiven
F# (D)   B (G)
 I have been set free
                F# (D)   E (C)
Through the blood of Jesus
F# (D)   G#m7 (Em7)
 I have been made clean
       F# (D)   E (C)
Now I know of His mercy because He died for me
                        B (G)
I have been redeemed

Taken from HOLY
Vineyard Music UK
VMUKCD06

Matt Redman

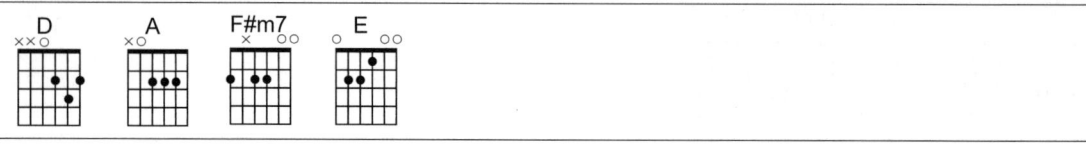

(Capo 2)

Verse 1:
```
        E (D)
When my heart runs dry
              B (A)
And there's no song to sing
          E (D)
No holy melody
          B (A)
No words of love within
 G#m7 (F#m7)            B (A)
I recall the height from which
    G#m7 (F#m7)      E (D)
This fragile heart has slipped
```

Chorus:
```
       B (A)        F# (E)
And I'll remember You
        G#m7 (F#m7)      E (D)          B (A)
I will turn back and do the things I used to do
       F# (E)
For the love of You
        B (A)        F# (E)
And I'll remember You
         G#m7 (F#m7)      E (D)          B (A)
I will turn back and do the things I used to do
       F# (E)       E (D)
For the love of You
```

Verse 2:
You are my soul's desire
You are the hope within
You bring my heart to life
You make my Spirit sing
I recall the height from which
This fragile heart has slipped

Taken from
WHERE ANGELS FEAR TO TREAD
Matt Redman
SURCD074

Dreamers Of Your Dreams   **Noel Richards & Ken Riley**

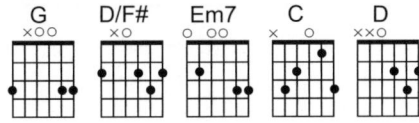

(Capo 3)

Chorus:
Bb (G)   F/A (D/F#)   Gm7 (Em7)   Eb (C)
  When we turn our hearts to heaven and bow down
Bb (G)   F/A (D/F#)   Gm7 (Em7)   Eb (C)
  We'll see fathers and the children reconciled
F (D)   Eb (C)   Bb (G)
 We'll be the dreamers of Your dreams
F (D)   Eb (C)   Bb (G)
 We'll be the dreamers of Your dreams

Verse 1:
Bb (G)   F/A (D/F#)   Gm7 (Em7)   Eb (C)
When Your fire falls from heaven we will rend our hearts to You
     Bb (G)   F/A (D/F#)   Gm7 (Em7)   Eb (C)
We will tell it to our children all the wonders You have done
     Bb (G)   F/A (D/F#)   Gm7 (Em7)   Eb (C)
And in every generation we will sing of Your great love
       Bb (G)   F/A (D/F#)   Gm7 (Em7)   Eb (C)
When Your fire falls from heaven we'll return to You again

Tag:
F (D)   Eb (C)   Bb (G)
 We'll be the dreamers of Your dreams
F (D)   Eb (C)   Bb (G)
 We'll be the dreamers of Your dreams

Taken from HURRICANE
The Hudson Taylors
KMCD2368

WHEN WORDS ARE NOT ENOUGH

I Surrender All

Martyn Layzell

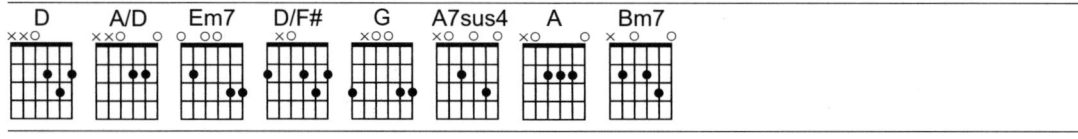

D   A/D   Em7   D/F#   G   A7sus4   A   Bm7

Capo 1

Verse 1:
```
        D         A/D   Em7
When words are not enough
D/F# G  D/F#        A7sus4    A
To tell of all You've done
D/F# G       D/F#       Em7   D/F#
 I   bow the knee, let silence speak
       G                 A7sus4    A
And gaze upon Your majesty
```

Verse 2:
These songs could not convey
A picture of Your love
And knowing this my life I give
To You an offering of praise

Chorus:
```
         D/F#  G  A7sus4
I surrender all
         D/F#  G  A7sus4
I surrender all
              Bm7
Unveil my heart to see
   G              A7sus4
The wonders of Your worth
             Em7    D/F#  G
As I surrender all
```

Verse 3:
The worship You require
Is brokenness of heart
So here I stand with open hands
Surrendered to Your love and power

Taken from
LOST IN WONDER
Martyn Layzell
SURCD076

WHEN WORDS ARE NOT ENOUGH

I Surrender All

Martyn Layzell

Verse 1:
```
     Eb         Bb/Eb  Fm7
When words are not enough
Eb/G Ab    Eb/G      Bb7sus4    Bb
  To  tell of all You've done
Eb/G Ab      Eb/G      Fm7    Eb/G
  I   bow the knee, let silence speak
     Ab                 Bb7sus4     Bb
And gaze upon Your majesty
```

Verse 2:
These songs could not convey
A picture of Your love
And knowing this my life I give
To You an offering of praise

Chorus:
```
           Eb/G  Ab  Bb7sus4
I surrender all
           Eb/G  Ab  Bb7sus4
I surrender all
                 Cm7
Unveil my heart to see
     Ab              Bb7sus4
The wonders of Your worth
                Fm7     Eb/G  Ab
As I surrender all
```

Verse 3:
The worship You require
Is brokenness of heart
So here I stand with open hands
Surrendered to Your love and power

Taken from
LOST IN WONDER
Martyn Layzell
SURCD076

WITH ALL MY HEART
171

Martyn Layzell & Mike Busbee

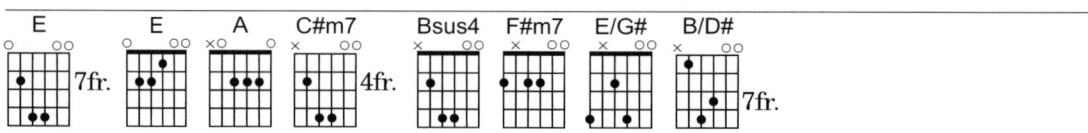

Verse 1:
```
      E             A          C#m7     A
With all my heart I say I love You
         E             A             C#m7     A
And it's my reward to stand before You
      Bsus4  A
With all my heart (with all my heart)
      Bsus4  A
With all my soul (with all my soul)
    F#m7  E/G#                A
With all my strength I worship You
```

Chorus:
```
          E         B/D#
You are my hearts desire
         C#m7      A
Nothing compares to You
         E      B/D#          F#m7     E/G#   A
Jesus my one desire, I worship You
         E      B/D#
Passionate hearts on fire
         C#m7      A
Sing in this place for You
         E      B/D#          F#m7     E/G#   A
Bowing before Your throne to honour You
```

Verse 2:
```
The life I live I'm living for You
With every breath I say I love You
With all my heart (with all my heart)
With all my soul (with all my soul)
With all my strength I worship You
```

Bridge:
```
     C#m7          A          E             A
Every nation, all of creation, every heart will sing Your praise
        C#m7          A          Bsus4
With celebration, songs of salvation bless Your name
        C#m7          A          E             A
Every nation, all of creation, every heart will sing Your praise
        C#m7          A          Bsus4
With celebration, songs of salvation we proclaim
```

Taken from
LOST IN WONDER
Martyn Layzell
SURCD076

WITH THE RENDING OF A HEART

172

Come Let Us Return

Matt Redman

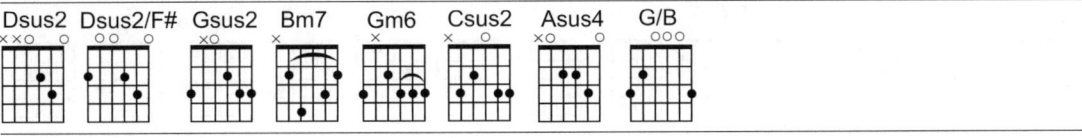

Dsus2 Dsus2/F# Gsus2 Bm7 Gm6 Csus2 Asus4 G/B

Chorus:
Dsus2 Dus2/F#   Gsus2
Come, come let us return to the Lord
Bm7   Dsus2/F#   Gsus2
Come, come let us return to the Lord
     Dsus2/F#   Gsus2
In brokenness of heart we consecrate our lives singing
Bm7   Dsus2/F#   Gsus2   Gm6
Come, come let us return to the Lord. (O) [Repeat x 5]

Verse:
Bm7   Dsus2   Gsus2   Bm7
    With the rending of a heart, with the bowing of a knee
Dsus2   Gsus2
Lord we are returning
Bm7   Dsus2   Gsus2   Bm7
    With a prayer and with a fast, with a song in minor key
Dsus2   Gsus2
Lord we are repenting
Em7   Dsus2/F#   Gsus2
    Even now,   even now, with all of our hearts
Em7   Dsus2/F#   Gsus2   Asus4
    You may turn,   You may leave a blessing behind. O, come...

Bridge:
Csus2   Gsus2
    In Your mercy You will come
                         Dsus2
In Your mercy You will come
Csus2   G/B
    Surely as the rising sun
                    Dsus2   [Asus4]
Surely as the rising sun

WONDERFUL REDEEMER

Ashton Gardner

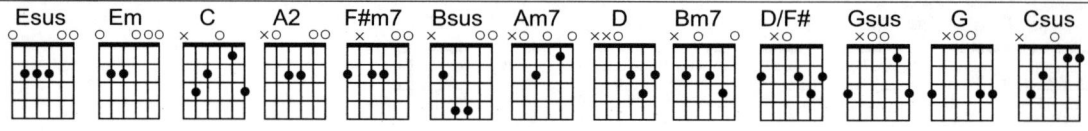

Esus   Em   C   A2   F#m7   Bsus   Am7   D   Bm7   D/F#   Gsus   G   Csus

Intro: Esus Em C A2   x2

Verse 1:
Esus   Em   C   F#m7
Wonderful redeemer of my life
Esus   Em   C   Bsus
Thank you for the grace You have shown to me
Esus   Em   Am7   D
Nothing can compare to Your heart of love
      Bm7   C
I have rest in Your arms

Chorus:
Em   D/F#   Am7
Sing to the Lord our God
   C   D   Gsus G
Lift up his name and exalt Him
Em   D/F#   Am7
Your holiness is unmatched
      C   D   Gsus G Csus   C   D Esus...intro
And we Your people will worship Your name forever

Verse 2:
Esus   Em   C   F#m7
Righteous and majestic King of truth
Esus   Em   C   Bsus
All mankind will one day bow their knees to You
Esus   Em   Am7   D
May our lives reflect the heart of You O Lord
      Bm7   C
We will live for You

Taken from the
INTERNATIONAL PEOPLE'S ALBUM
Soul Survivor
SURCD054

WONDERFUL SO WONDERFUL

Beautiful One

Tim Hughes

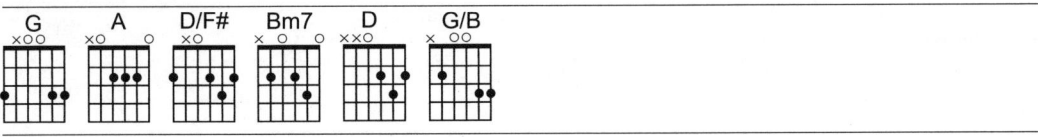

G   A   D/F#   Bm7   D   G/B

Verse 1:
```
G              A           D/F#
Wonderful, so wonderful, is Your unfailing love
     G            A         Bm7
Your cross has spoken mercy over me
   G           A              D/F#
No eye has seen, no ear has heard, no heart could fully know
   G          A          D
How glorious, how beautiful You are
```

Chorus:
```
        G     A
Beautiful one I love You
        G     A
Beautiful one I adore
        G      A        D
Beautiful one my soul must sing
```

Verse 2:
```
Powerful, so powerful, Your glory fills the skies
Your mighty works displayed for all to see
The beauty of Your majesty, awakes my heart to sing
How marvelous, how wonderful You are
```

Bridge:
```
     G                     A
You opened my eyes to Your wonders anew
     G                     A
You captured my heart with this love
       G                  A          D
'Cause nothing on earth is as beautiful as You    (repeat)
```

Coda:
```
     G              A
My soul my soul must sing
   G/B              A/C#
My soul my soul must sing
     G              A
My soul my soul must sing
         D
Beautiful one
```

Taken from
GLIMPSES OF GLORY
Soul Survivor Live 2002
SURCD082

WORTHY, YOU ARE WORTHY

Worthy

Matt Redman

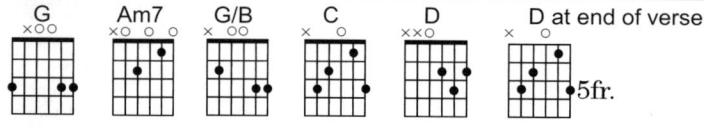

(Capo 4)

Verse 1:
```
  B (G)              C#m7 (Am7)
Worthy, You are worthy
            B/D# (G/B)      E (C)
Much more worthy than I know
B (G)       C#m7 (Am7)
I cannot imagine
            B/D# (G/B)   E (C)
Just how glorious You are
F# (D)           E (C)
And I cannot begin to tell
       B/D# (G/B)              E (C)
How deep the love You bring
F# (D)                     E (C)
O Lord, my ears have heard of You
   B/D# (G/B)          E (C)  F# (D)  E (C)  F# (D)  E(C)
But now my eyes have seen
```

Chorus:
```
        B (G)           C#m7 (Am7)
You're worthy, You're worthy
        B/D# (G/B)     E (C)
You're worthy
        B (G)           C#m7 (Am7)
You're worthy to be praised
   B/D# (G/B)        E (C)
Forever and a day          (rpt)
```

Verse 2:
Glory, I give glory to the One who saved my soul
You found me and You freed me from the shame that was my own
And I cannot begin to tell how merciful You've been
O Lord, my ears have heard of You but now my eyes have seen

Chorus 2: (high)
You're worthy, You're worthy, You're worthy
You're worthy to be praised, forever and a day
Your glory, Your glory, Your glory
Your glory reaches high, so high above the heavens

Taken from GRACE
Live Worship from New Wine 2001
KMCD2335

All That Matters

Eoghan Heaslip

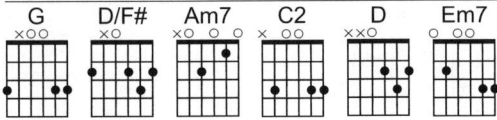

G   D/F#   Am7   C2   D   Em7

Chorus:
G   D/F#
You are all that matters
          Am7
All that satisfies
          C2
All that gives me life
D   G
And stands the test of time
          D/F#
You are my portion
         Am7
My only passion
        C2   D   Em7 C2
You mean everything to me
   D   G
Everything

Verse 1:
  C2   G
I give You all I have
       Em7   D/F#
Lord I love You and adore You
   C2   G
I come just as I am
      Em7   D/F#
To worship with my whole heart
C2   D
Jesus, Jesus

Verse 2:
Lord my life is in Your hands
Would You fashion, would You form me
Fulfill Your purpose and Your plan
I'm surrendered to Your ways

Tag:
 D   G   D/F#
You are all that, all that, all that matters
Em7   C2
All that, all that matters   (repeat)

Taken from
MERCY
Eoghan Heaslip
Hosanna 22482

YOU ARE GOD IN HEAVEN

Let My Words Be Few

Matt & Beth Redman

G   Gaug   Em   C2   Am7   G/B   D   F2   A7sus4

Verse 1:
```
G                 Gaug
  You are God in heaven
      Em          C2
And here am I on earth
G      Gaug          Em    C2
  So I'll let my words be few
Am7 G/B  C2    D       G
Jesus I am so in love with You
```

Chorus:
```
        G      F2     Em    A7sus4    C2
And I'll stand in awe of You
        G      F2     Em    C2
Yes I'll stand in awe of You
        Am7    G/B    C2
And I'll let my words be few
Am7 G/B  C2    D       G
Jesus I am so in love with You
```

Verse 2:
The simplest of all love songs
I want to bring to You
So I'll let my words be few
Jesus I am so in love with You

Taken from
GLIMPSES OF GLORY
Soul Survivor Live 2002
SURCD082
and The Father's Song
Matt Redman
SURCD038

YOU ARE HOLY

Trè Sheppard

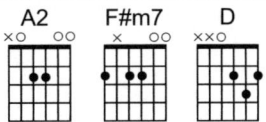

A2   F#m7   D

Intro: A2   F#m7   D   A2   x2

Chorus:
```
        A2              F#m7
You are holy, You are mercy
        D               A2
You are wonder, You are love
        A2              F#m7
You are faithful, You are gracious
        D               A2
You are lovely, You are God
```


Verse 1:
```
F#m7   D        F#m7      D
I open my eyes so I see Your loveliness
F#m7   D        F#m7      D
I open my life so I know Your holiness
```


Verse 2:
```
If You are for us who could stand against us?
And surely You are with us, surely You are with us
```


Tag:
```
F#m7   D
Surely You are with us
F#m7   D
Surely You are with us
F#m7   D
Surely You are with us
F#m7   D
Surely You are with us
```

Taken from CARDIPHONIA
100 Hours
SURCD073

YOU ARE THE LORD

Famous One

Chris Tomlin & Jesse Reeves

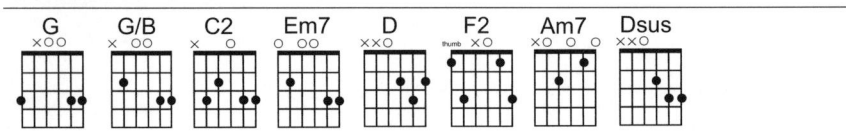

Chorus:
```
  G          G/B        C2
You are the Lord the famous One, famous One
  Em7          D          C2
Great is Your name in all the earth
        G      G/B        C2
The heavens declare You're glorious, glorious
  Em7        D          G    G/B   F2    C2
Great is Your fame beyond the earth
```

Verse 1:
```
        Am7             G/B
And for all You've done and yet to do
        C2             G
With every breath I'm praising You
          Am7       G/B
Desire of nations and every heart
        C2           Dsus
You alone are God, You alone are God
```

Verse 2:
```
The morning star is shining through
And every eye is watching You
Revealed by nature and miracles
You are beautiful, You are beautiful
```

Taken from OUR LOVE IS LOUD
Passion
SPD51923

YOU ARE THE LORD

180

Glorious

Eoghan Heaslip & Mike Goss

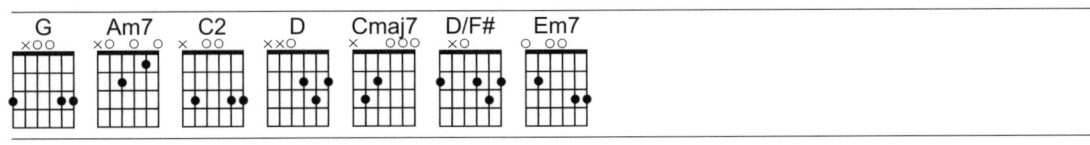

Capo 1

Intro: G   Am7   C2   D   x4

Verse 1:
G   Am7   C2   D
  You are the Lord, the King of Heaven
G   Am7   C2   D
  And all the earth, You'll reign forever
G   Am7   C2 D   G   Am7   C2   D
  First and the last,   You are glorious
G   Am7   C2   D
  Before Your throne the elders fall
G   Am7 C2   D
  And angels sing "Almighty God"
G   Am7   C2   D
  Bright morning star
     Cmaj7   D   Cmaj7   D
You are   glorious, You are   glorious

Chorus 1:
  G   D/F#
To You the nations will come
    Am7   C2   D
Every tribe, every tongue and worship before
  G   D/F#   Am7
You, the Ancient of Days, the Name above all names
    C2   D   Em7
Who is worthy of all our praise
  C2   D   G
You are glorious

Chorus 2:
  G   D/F#
To You the nations will come
    Am7   C2   D
Every tribe every tongue and worship before
  G   D/F#   Am7
You, the Ancient of Days, the Name above all names
    C2   D
Who is worthy of praise...   (to Chorus 1)

Taken from
MERCY
Eoghan Heaslip
Hosanna 22482

YOU ARE THE LORD

Glorious

180

Eoghan Heaslip & Mike Goss

Intro: Ab   Bbm7   Db   Eb   x4

Verse 1:
Ab   Bbm7   Db   Eb
    You are the Lord, the King of Heaven
Ab   Bbm7   Db   Eb
    And all the earth, You'll reign forever
Ab   Bbm7   Db   Eb   Ab   Bbm7   Db   Eb
    First and the last,   You are glorious
Ab   Bbm7   Db   Eb
    Before Your throne the elders fall
Ab   Bbm7   Db   Eb
    And angels sing "Almighty God"
Ab   Bbm7   Db   Eb
    Bright morning star
       Dbmaj7   Eb   Dbmaj7   Eb
You are   glorious, You are   glorious

Chorus 1:
    Ab   Eb/G
To You the nations will come
      Bbm7   Db   Eb
Every tribe, every tongue and worship before
 Ab   Eb/G   Bbm7
You, the Ancient of Days, the Name above all names
        Db   Eb   Fm7
Who is worthy of all our praise
Db   Eb   Ab
You are glorious

Chorus 2:
    Ab   Eb/G
To You the nations will come
      Bbm7   Db   Eb
Every tribe every tongue and worship before
 Ab   Eb/G   Bbm7
You, the Ancient of Days, the Name above all names
        Db   Eb
Who is worthy of praise...   (to Chorus 1)

Taken from
MERCY
Eoghan Heaslip
Hosanna 22482

YOU ARE THE ONE

God Is Still For Us

Johnny Parks

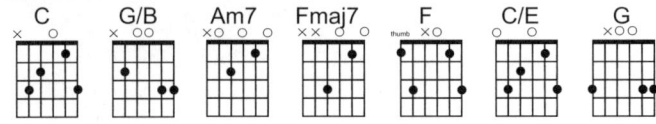

C   G/B   Am7   Fmaj7   F   C/E   G

(Capo 4)

Intro: E (C)   B/D# (G/B)   C#m7 (Am7)   Amaj7 (Fmaj7)   x2

Verse 1:
```
          E (C)                Amaj7 (Fmaj7)
You are the One who gave His Son
     E (C)          Amaj7 (Fmaj7)
Who freely gave us all things
     C#m7 (Am7)      A (F)           E (C)         Amaj7 (Fmaj7)
And nothing can be against us if God is still for us
     E (C)               Amaj7 (Fmaj7)
And all things work for good
     E (C)               Amaj7 (Fmaj7)
For those who love the Lord
     C#m7 (Am7)      A (F)           E (C)       A (F)
And nothing can be against us if God is still for us
```

Pre-Chorus:
```
          A (F)          E/G# (C/E)      B (G)
And we're convinced that neither death nor life
          E (C)         A (F)
Nor angels nor demons, nor height nor depth
     E/G# (C/E)              B (G)                 A (F)
Or what's to come, can cut us off from the love of God
```

Chorus:
```
          E (C)           B/D# (G/B)         C#m7 (Am7)
God is still for us, God is still for us, God is still for us
          A (F)
Turn around          (rpt)
```

Verse 2:
When hardship or danger comes
We know that God gave His only Son
So as a body we are assured that God is still for us
We look to You Lord, we stand on Your word
We're holding on to the promise You've made
That nothing can be against us if God is still for us

Alternative Chorus:
```
     C#m7 (Am7)        B/D# (G/B)            E (C)
God is still for us, God is still for us, God is still for us
          B (G) - A (F) on rpt
Turn around                (rpt)
```

Taken from CLOSE TO YOU
Johnny Parks
SURCD055

(no capo)

Intro: Dm7 C/E F   Dm7 C/E Bb

Verse:
Dm7 C/E   F   Dm7
You call us first to love Your name
      C/E   Bb
To worship You
Dm7 C/E   F   Dm7   C/E
To   please Your heart, our one desire
       Bb
Oh Lord

Chorus:
F   C/E   Dm7
If there's one thing we are called to do
      Bb F   Bb   C
It's to love You, to adore You
F   C/E   Dm7
We will bring our all and worship You
      Bb F   Bb   C
Bow before You as we love You

Verse 2:
Your honour Lord Your name's renown
We long to see
So let the glory of Your name
Be praised

Bridge:
Am7   Bb
I will celebrate this love
                       F C/E Dm7
Jesus You are everything to   me
Am7   Bb
For what more Lord can I do
                     F C/E Dm7   Bb
I will give this heart this life to   You

Taken from HERE I AM TO WORSHIP
Tim Hughes
SURCD053

YOU CALL US FIRST

One Thing

Tim Hughes

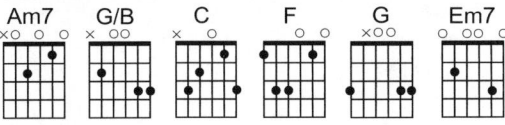

(Capo 5)

Intro: Am7 G/B C   Am7 G/B F

Verse:
Am7 G/B   C   Am7
You call us first to love Your name
      G/B   F
To worship You
Am7 G/B   C   Am7 G/B
To   please Your heart our one desire
      F
Oh Lord

Chorus:
C   G/B   Am7
If there's one thing we are called to do
      F   C   F   G
It's to love You, to adore You
C   G/B   Am7
We will bring our all and worship You
      F   C   F   G
Bow before You as we love You

Verse 2:
Your honour Lord Your name's renown
We long to see
So let the glory of Your name
Be praised

Bridge:
Em7   F
I will celebrate this love
                    C G/B Am7
Jesus You are everything to me
Em7   F
For what more Lord can I do
                    C G/B Am7 F
I will give this heart this life to   You

Taken from HERE I AM TO WORSHIP
Tim Hughes
SURCD053

YOU CAN HAVE MY WHOLE LIFE

I Want To Go Your Way

183

James Taylor

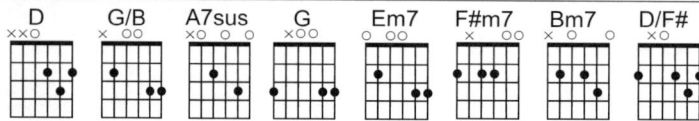

D   G/B   A7sus   G   Em7   F#m7   Bm7   D/F#

(Capo 3)

Verse 1:
F (D)   Bb/D (G/B)
You can have my whole life
       C (A7sus)   Bb (G)
You can come and have it all
     Gm7 (Em7)   C (A7sus) F (D)
I don't want to go my own way now

Verse 2:
F (D)   Bb/D (G/B)
I love to feel Your presence
       C (A7sus)   Bb (G)
And I know Your saving grace
     Gm7 (Em7)   C (A7sus) F (D)
I am nothing when You're second   place

Chorus:
Am7 (F#m7) Bb (G)   F (D)
I've been   born to give You praise
     Am7 (F#m7)   Dm7 (Bm7)
Not to yearn and strive for worldly things
     Bb (G)   F/A (D/F#)
I've been born to love Your ways
      Am7 (F#m7)   Gm7 (Em7)
Take my pride and let me always say
       C (A7sus) F (D)
I want to go Your way now

Taken from the
INTERNATIONAL PEOPLE'S ALBUM
Soul Survivor
SURCD054

YOU CAN SHINE LIGHT

184

Nothing Is Impossible

Vicky Beeching

C	Em7	D	G/B	Am7	G	D/F#

Capo 3

Intro: C   Em7 D   C   Em7 D   (repeat)

Verse 1:
```
 C    Em7 D      C            G/B
You can        shine light into the darkness
     C    Em7 D   G/B         C
And You can        set every prisoner free
     C    Em7 D      C            G/B
And You can        make streams flow in the desert
     C    Em7 D   G/B         C
And this        is what we are longing to see
   Am7     G/B    C
Because we know and we believe...
```


Chorus:
```
Em7      C        G          D/F#
Nothing, nothing is impossible for You
Em7        C         G              D/F#
Anything, anything can happen when Your power breaks through
Em7        C       G          D/F#
Send Your power and let Your will be done
        Am7    C      D      C
God of miracles let Your kingdom come
```


Verse 2:
Come Lord, shine light into the darkness
Come Lord, set every prisoner free
Come Lord, make streams flow in the desert
'Cause this is what we are longing to see
Because we know and we believe...

n.b.   when repeating a chorus the last line is;
        "God of miracles, we believe that..."

Taken from
ON THE STREETS
Festival Manchester
SURCD095

YOU CAN SHINE LIGHT

184

Nothing Is Impossible

Vicky Beeching

Intro: Eb   Gm7 F   Eb   Gm7 F   (repeat)

Verse 1:
```
 Eb    Gm7  F     Eb          Bb/D
You can        shine light into the darkness
      Eb   Gm7  F   Bb/D        Eb
And You can        set every prisoner free
      Eb   Gm7  F     Eb          Bb/D
And You can        make streams flow in the desert
     Eb Gm7 F      Bb/D           Eb
And this       is what we are longing to see
     Cm7    Bb/D   Eb
Because we know and we believe...
```

Chorus:
```
Gm7     Eb        Bb       F/A
Nothing, nothing is impossible for You
Gm7     Eb        Bb           F/A
Anything, anything can happen when Your power breaks through
Gm7     Eb      Bb        F/A
Send Your power and let Your will be done
       Cm7    Eb      F      Eb
God of miracles let Your kingdom come
```

Verse 2:
```
Come Lord, shine light into the darkness
Come Lord, set every prisoner free
Come Lord, make streams flow in the desert
'Cos this is what we are longing to see
Because we know and we believe...
```

n.b.   when repeating a chorus the last line is;
       "God of miracles, we believe that..."

Taken from
ON THE STREETS
Festival Manchester
SURCD095

YOU CHOSE THE CROSS

185

Lost In Wonder

Martyn Layzell

G   D/F#   Em7   C   D   Am7   G/B

(Capo 3)

Verse 1:
    Bb (G)   F/A (D/F#)
You chose the cross with every breath
    Gm7 (Em7)
The perfect life, the perfect death
Eb (C)   Bb (G)   F (D)
      You chose the cross
  Bb (G)   F/A (D/F#)
A crown of thorns You wore for us
    Gm7 (Em7)
And crowned us with eternal life
Eb (C)   Bb (G)   F (D)
      You chose the cross
    Cm7 (Am7)   Bb/D (G/B)   F (D)
And though Your soul was overwhelmed with pain
  Cm7 (Am7) Bb/D (G/B)   F (D)
Obedient to death, You overcame

Chorus:
        Bb (G)
I'm lost in wonder
        Gm7 (Em7)
I'm lost in love
        Eb (C)   F (D)
I'm lost in praise for evermore
        Bb (G)   Gm7 (Em7)
Because of Jesus' unfailing love
        Eb (C)
I am forgiven
        F (D)
I am restored

Verse 2:
You loosed the cords of sinfulness
And broke the chains of my disgrace
You chose the cross
Up from the grave victorious
You rose again so glorious
You chose the cross
The sorrow that surrounded you was mine
"Yet not my will but Yours be done" You cried

Taken from
LOST IN WONDER
Martyn Layzell
SURCD076

YOU FORMED US FROM THE DUST 186

Created To Worship

Vicky Beeching

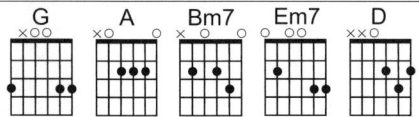

G   A   Bm7   Em7   D

Capo 2

Verse 1:
G   A   Bm7
  You formed us from the dust
G   A   Bm7
  You breathed Your breath in us
G   A   Bm7   Em7
  We are the work of Your hands
G   A   Bm7
  Now we breathe back to You
G   A   Bm7
  Love songs of gratitude
G A   Bm7   Em7
  Adoring You with all we have

Chorus:
            G   Bm7 A   D   G   Bm7   A
We were created   to worship Your name
D   G   Bm7 A   D   G   Bm7   A
We were created   to bring You our praise
 D   G   Bm7 A D   G   Bm7 A
So we will worship,   so we will praise
D   Em7   D/F#   G
You our creator   for all our days

Verse 2:
If we don't worship You
We'll search for substitutes
To fill the void in our hearts
Worshiping other things
Destroys our liberty
But as we praise You we are free

Bridge:
   G   Bm7
For this is what we were made to do   (repeat line x3)
G   A
So we lift up our praise to You

Taken from SHELTER
Vicky Beeching
SURCD083

Created To Worship — **Vicky Beeching**

Verse 1:
```
A      B          C#m7
 You formed us from the dust
A      B          C#m7
 You breathed Your breath in us
A    B    C#m7        F#m7
 We are the work of Your hands
A      B          C#m7
 Now we breathe back to You
A      B          C#m7
 Love songs of gratitude
A  B   C#m7           F#m7
 Adoring You with all we have
```

Chorus:
```
            A   C#m7  B   E           A      C#m7  B
We were created            to worship Your name
 E       A   C#m7  B   E           A      C#m7  B
We were created            to bring You our praise
 E       A   C#m7  B   E    A     C#m7  B
So we will worship,        so we will praise
 E      F#m7   E/G#     A
You our creator        for all our days
```

Verse 2:
If we don't worship You
We'll search for substitutes
To fill the void in our hearts
Worshiping other things
Destroys our liberty
But as we praise You we are free

Bridge:
```
   A                  C#m7
For this is what we were made to do    (repeat x3)
A              B
So we lift up our praise to You
```

Taken from SHELTER
Vicky Beeching
SURCD083

YOU GAVE YOUR ONLY SON

Praise You

Martyn Layzell

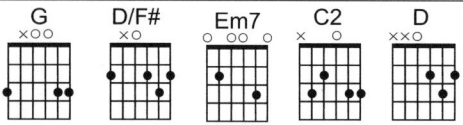

G   D/F#   Em7   C2   D

Verse 1:
G
You gave Your only son
D/F#
Came down from heaven above
Em7   C2
Endured the cross so I might know
G
This love that reached for me
D/F#
A love that sets me free
Em7   C2
Your sacrifice has saved my soul

Pre-Chorus:
Em7   D/F#   G   C2
     Today I'm reminded of Your grace
Em7   D/F#   G   C2   D   C2
     Always living now to sing Your praise, Your praise

Chorus:
G   Em7
Praise You, Jesus I praise You
  C2   D   C2
I lift my hands and sing
     G   Em7
Embrace You, I will embrace You
  C2   D   C2
Saviour and my King, my King

Verse 2:
I could not earn this
Such undeserved love
Jesus I know You are the way
You paid the price for me
Your blood was shed for me
And in Your mercy took my place

Taken from
LOST IN WONDER
Martyn Layzell
SURCD076

YOU HAVE BEEN SO GOOD TO ME

188

Trè & Tori Sheppard

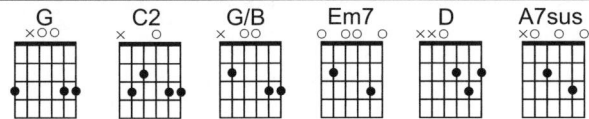

Intro: G C2 G C2   G C2 G C2

Verse 1:
```
        G G/B C2          G G/B C2
You have been      so good to me
        G G/B C2          G G/B C2
You have been      so good to me
Em7    D  C2   E m7   D  C2   G
Love is so fine, love is all mine
Em7    D  C2
All of my life I'll live
   A7sus G/B  C2                   G  C2  G  C2
To have Your heart and give You mine
```

Verse 2:
```
You have been so good to me
You have been so good to me
Love is so fine, love is all mine
All of my life I'll live
To find Your heart like You found mine
```

Verse 3/Outro:
```
Em7     D  C2  Em7   D  C2
Love is so fine, love is all mine
Em7        D  C2
And all of my life I'll live
   A7sus G/B  C2            A7sus
To have Your heart, I want to have
 G/B  C2       A7sus    G/B C2     A7sus  G/B  C2
Your heart, could I have Your heart?
                 G  G/B  C2
'Cause You have mine
                    G  G/B  C2
Yeah You have mine
```

Taken from CARDIPHONIA
100 Hours
SURCD073

YOU HAVE QUIETED
Shouts Of Joy

Sarah Yeager

E   C#m7   A2   Bsus

Verse 1:
E
You have quieted the raging of the oceans
E
Along with their waves
E
You have silenced the shouting of the nations
E
Every land will bow

Pre-Chorus:
  C#m7   A2
Even those who live at the ends of the world
           E
They will stand in awe of You
            C#m7   A2
From when the sun rises 'til it sets again
Bsus A2   E   A2   E   A2
You inspire shouts of joy

Chorus:
         E   A2
And the singers they will sing
        E   A2
As the peoples they draw near
         E   A2
Now the dancers they will dance
        E   A2
Let Your music play on and on

Verse 2:
We'll rejoice when the unjust is avenged
For our God, He is just
At His feet every knee will bow down
As we humbly praise

Taken from the
INTERNATIONAL PEOPLE'S ALBUM
Soul Survivor
SURCD054

YOU MADE A PERFECT WORLD

Everything Changed At The Cross

David Gate

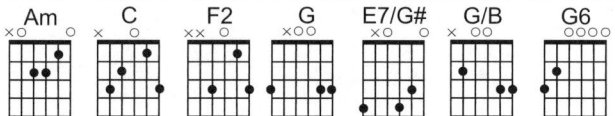

Verse 1:
Am   C
   You made a perfect world and saw that it was good
Am   F2
   And You dwelt there in that place
Am   C
   But through the sin of man it became a fallen world
Am   F2
   And we no longer saw Your face

Pre-Chorus:
                   G   F2
But through the power of grace
      G   F2
You restored the way
      G   E7/G#
Jesus You have brought us home

Chorus:
  Am   G/B   F2   G
Everything changed at the cross
  Am   G/B   F2   G
Everything changed at the cross
  Am   G/B
Death became life
  C   F2
Night became day
  G
Your kingdom came and
E7/G#   Am G6 F2 G6   Am G6 F2 G6
Everything changed at the cross

Verse 2:
We were a hopeless race condemned to our disgrace
But You chose to intervene laying down Your life
A perfect sacrifice to make the Father's love complete

YOU POUR OUT GRACE

Gareth Robinson & Joannah Oyeniran

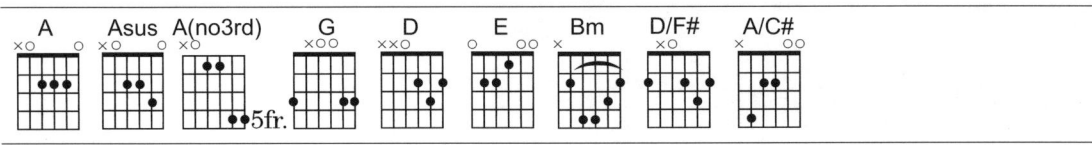

Verse 1:

```
A              Asus         A(no3rd)  Asus
  You pour out grace on the broken     hearted
A              Asus         A(no3rd)  Asus
  And You lift the hope of the weary      soul
        G                              D          A  Asus  A(no3rd)  Asus
And You  stretch out Your hand with Your loving mercy
A              Asus         A(no3rd)  Asus
  You saw this heart that was lost and   broken
A              Asus         A(no3rd)  Asus
  And You felt the pain of my loneli  -  ness
        G                    D          A  Asus  A(no3rd)  Asus
And You  befriended me and restored my dignity
```

Chorus:

```
  A     E    Bm            D
You alone revealed the love of God to me
        A    E     G    D/F#
And You alone have given everything for me
        A    E    Bm      A/C#   D     A  Asus  A(no3rd)  Asus
And You alone deserve the highest praise Jesus
```

Verse 2:
You demonstrated the life of love to me
And how it was that You wanted me to live
Heart of compassion and hands of healing
I need Your Spirit to help accomplish this
Abundant grace and Your strength in weakness
And the steady hand of the Father holding me

Bridge:

```
Bm              A/C#       D     E
   And You have given me great salvation
Bm              A/C#    D     E
And You have given me hope eternal
  Bm      A/C#   D     E
And everyday I look to give You
Bm       A/C#       D         E
   All the glory that's due Your name
```

Taken from GRACE
Live Worship from New Wine 2001
KMCD2335

YOU SHAPED THE HEAVENS

Maker Of All Things

Tim Hughes

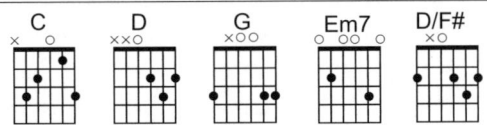

C   D   G   Em7   D/F#

Intro: C   D G   C   D G   C   D G   C

Verse:
```
C                   D              C
You shaped the heavens and the earth
            Em7 D  C
Revealed your splendour
                    G       D       C
You spoke Your life into our hearts
            Em7  D  C
So we belong to You
```

Chorus:
```
              C        D    G
You are the Maker of all things
    C              D
First and the Last
        C          D   G        C
Creation sings praise to You God
              C       D  G
You're reigning in glory
      C            D
Ancient of Days
            C        D   G        C
Your people sing praise to You God
```

Verse 2:
Creator God in You all things
Have come together
Working Your wonders day by day
You'll reign forever

Tag:
```
        D/F#                G
And earth joins with Heaven,
      C
Declaring Your Glory,
        D/F#        Em7              C
Proclaiming the works of Your hands    (repeat)
```

YOU SPREAD OUT THE SKIES

Wonderful Maker

Matt Redman & Chris Tomlin

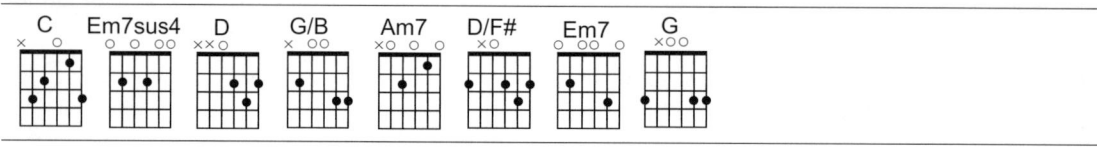

Verse 1:
C
You spread out the skies over empty space
Em7sus4
Said "let there be light" to a dark and formless world
               C   D
Your light was born

Verse 2:
G/B C
   You spread out Your arms over empty hearts
Em7sus4
Said "let there be light" to a dark and hopeless world
             C   D
Your Son was born

Pre-Chorus:
   Am7   G/B   C
You made the world and saw that it was good
   Am7   G/B   C   D/F#
You sent Your only Son for You are good

Chorus:
                      C   Em7
What a wonderful maker, what a wonderful Saviour
              C   D/F#   G
How majestic Your whispers, and how humble Your love
               G/B   C   Em7
With a strength like no other, and the heart of a Father
              C   D/F#   G or (Am7 G/B C...)
How majestic Your whispers, what a wonderful God

Verse 3:
No eye has fully seen how beautiful the cross
And we have only heard the faintest whisper of how great You are

Taken from
WHERE ANGELS FEAR TO TREAD
Matt Redman
SURCD074

YOU'VE GIVEN ME PASSION

Hands Up

Ken Riley

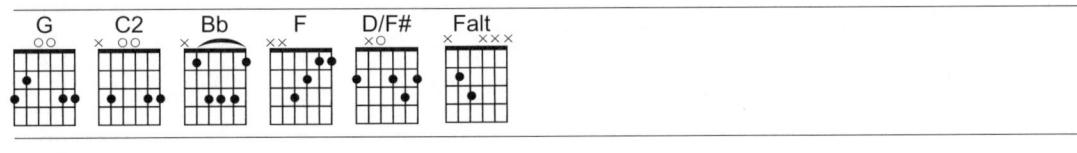

Intro: G   Falt   C   F   G   Falt   C   F

Verse 1:
       G   C2   G   C2
You've given me passion   burning within my heart
     G   C2
Unspoken expressions of worship created
     G   C2
To lift You up
G7   C
I know words can't declare the feelings
G7   C2
 I bring to You
G7   C2   G7   C2
I will climb to the highest heavens   for one glimpse of You
        Bb   C
With everything I worship You

Chorus:
G   C
 I lift my hands up,   lift my hands up
F   D/F#
 I lift my hands to You
G   C
  Open my heart up,   open my heart
      F
Declare that it's true
         D/F#   G
There is no one who loves like You

[After Chorus 2 and End]
        G Falt C   F
Lift your hands up.

Verse 2:
Now I have Jesus, living within my heart
I've opened this temple of worship created
To bring You love
I know words can't declare the feelings
I bring to You
I will climb to the highest heavens for one glimpse of You
With everything I worship You

Bridge:
G   C2   (F)
Lord I lift my hands, Lord I lift my hands
G   C2 (F)
Lord I lift my hands to You

Taken from
REVOLUTION
YFriday
SURCD093

YOUR HAND HAS LIFTED ME

Shine Like The Stars

Paul Oakley

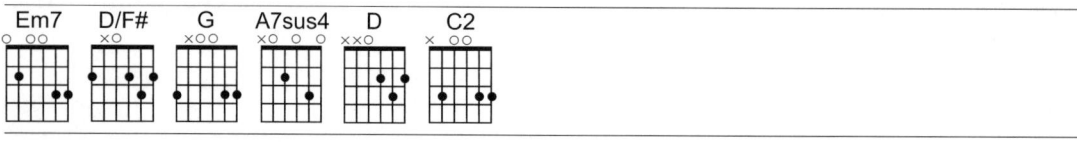

Capo 2

Verse 1:
```
Em7              D/F#            G
   Your hand has lifted me from death
Em7          D/F#        C2
   You set my feet on solid ground
Em7          D/F#              G           D/F#      C2
   You put a song in my heart and crown me with Your love
   A7sus4     C2    D
My Saviour, my God
```

Verse 2:
You give me dignity and grace
Beauty for ashes, love for hate
You meet my every need, Your mercy fills my soul
Until I overflow

Chorus:
```
          Em7 D/F# C2        Em7         D/F# C2
Help me to shine,        help me to shine like the stars above
          Em7      D/F# C2         A7sus4 C2          Em7...
Help me to live like the one I love, help me to shine,      help me to shine
```

Verse 3:
I need to share this love I've found
Many are those with broken hearts
Send me to bind up their wounds and comfort those who grieve
My Jesus, set them free

Chorus 2:
Help me to shine, help me to shine like the stars above
Help me to love those who have no love, help me to shine

Bridge:
```
          Em7  D/F#  C2
Because freely I've received
          Em7      D/F#    C2
And Your love has captured me
          Em7  D/F#  G             A7sus4    C2
So compel me Lord to give Your love away
```

Taken from
ON THE STREETS
Festival Manchester 2003
SURCD095
and
BE LIFTED UP
Paul Oakley
SURCD085

YOUR HAND HAS LIFTED ME

Shine Like The Stars

Verse 1:
F#m7   E/G#   A
    Your hand has lifted me from death
F#m7   E/G#   D2
    You set my feet on solid ground
F#m7   E/G#   A   E/G#   D2
     You put a song in my heart and crown me with Your love
   B7sus4   D2   E
My Saviour, my God

Verse 2:
You give me dignity and grace
Beauty for ashes, love for hate
You meet my every need, Your mercy fills my soul
Until I overflow

Chorus:
      F#m7 E/G# D2   F#m7   E/G# D2
Help me to shine,   help me to shine like the stars above
      F#m7   E/G# D2   B7sus4 D2   F#m7...
Help me to live like the one I love, help me to shine,   help me to shine

Verse 3:
I need to share this love I've found
Many are those with broken hearts
Send me to bind up their wounds and comfort those who grieve
My Jesus, set them free

Chorus 2:
Help me to shine, help me to shine like the stars above
Help me to love those who have no love, help me to shine

Bridge:
     F#m7 E/G# D2
Because freely I've received
      F#m7 E/G#   D2
And Your love has captured me
     F#m7 E/G# A   B7sus4   D2
So compel me Lord to give Your love away

Taken from
ON THE STREETS
Festival Manchester 2003
SURCD095
and
BE LIFTED UP
Paul Oakley
SURCD085

YOUR KINDNESS

Wonderful, Beautiful, Merciful

(no capo)

```
Intro:   F : A    Dm : Bb    C    C : Bb
         F : A    Dm : Bb    C    C : Bb
```

Verse 1:
```
F                          Fmaj7
Your kindness overwhelmed me, the love that captured me
    Bb      F/A  Gm7       Eb   Bb/D   Csus    C
You helped me to believe that You delight in me
F                          Fmaj7
You led me to the Father, and introduced us there
    Bb      F/A    Gm7       Eb     Bb/D      Csus    C
The Spirit poured out grace and filled me with Your praise
```

Chorus:
```
              F       A      Dm
You are wonderful, beautiful, merciful
 Bb           F     Csus          F     Csus
And all my life and my heart belong to You         (rpt)
```

Verse 2:
Your plans for me are greater than I have ever thought
You're daily changing me, revealing more to me
My love for You is growing and as I reach for You
The Spirit poured out grace and filled me with Your praise

Taken from IS IT ANY WONDER
Heat
SURCD071

YOUR KINDNESS

Wonderful, Beautiful, Merciful

James Gregory

D	F#	Bm	G	A	Dmaj7	D/F#	Em7	C	G/B	Asus

(Capo 3)

Intro: D : F#   Bm : G   A   A : G
            D : F#   Bm : G   A   A : G

Verse 1:
D   Dmaj7
Your kindness overwhelmed me, the love that captured me
      G   D/F# Em7   C   G/B   Asus   A
You helped me to believe that You delight in me
D   Dmaj7
You led me to the Father, and introduced us there
        G   D/F# Em7   C   G/B   Asus   A
The Spirit poured out grace and filled me with Your praise

Chorus:
           D   F#   Bm
You are wonderful, beautiful, merciful
 G   D   Asus   D   Asus
And all my life and my heart belong to You   (rpt)

Verse 2:
Your plans for me are greater than I have ever thought
You're daily changing me, revealing more to me
My love for You is growing and as I reach for You
The Spirit poured out grace and filled me with Your praise

Taken from IS IT ANY WONDER
Heat
SURCD071

YOUR MERCY FALLS

Ken Riley & Jane Kitson

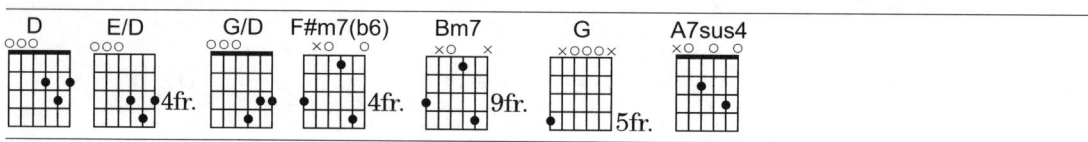

Capo 2 - (tune low E down to D)

Verse 1:
```
        D            E/D
Your mercy falls into this place
        G/D              D
Salvation dawns with Your embrace
        D            E/D
Waves of love flow from Your mountain
        G/D              D
Cleansing tears fall like rain
```

Chorus:
```
F#m7b6  Bm7  G            A7sus4
Je - sus, restorer of my soul
F#m7b6  Bm7    G            A7sus4
    I find forgiveness at Your throne
F#m7b6  Bm7    G         A7sus4    G       D
    I come to worship and adore my God
```

```
  G       D
Halle, Hallelujah
  G       D
Halle, Hallelujah
  G       D
Halle, Hallelujah
  G       D
Halle, Hallelujah      (repeat as necessary)
```

Taken from
SONGS OF HEAVEN
YFriday
YFCD02

Ken Riley & Jane Kitson

Verse 1:
```
             F              G/F
Your mercy falls into this place
             Bb/F                F
Salvation dawns with Your embrace
             F              G/F
Waves of love flow from Your mountain
             Bb/F        F
Cleansing tears fall like rain
```

Chorus:
```
Am7  Dm9  Bb          Csus4
Je - sus,  restorer of my soul
Am7  Dm9    Bb              Csus4
    I find forgiveness at Your throne
Am7  Dm9     Bb          Csus4     Bb       F
    I come to worship and adore my God
```

```
  Bb         F
Halle, Hallelujah
  Bb         F
Halle, Hallelujah
  Bb         F
Halle, Hallelujah
  Bb         F
Halle, Hallelujah      (repeat as necessary)
```

Taken from
SONGS OF HEAVEN
YFriday
YFCD02

YOUR VOICE IS

Awesome God

Vicky Beeching

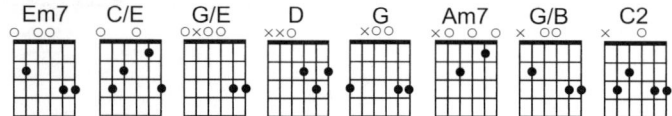

Em7   C/E   G/E   D   G   Am7   G/B   C2

Intro: Em7   C/E   G/E   D   x2

Verse 1:
Em7　　　　C/E
　　Your voice is the voice that
G　　　　　　　D
　Commanded the universe to be
Em7　　　　　　C/E
　　Your voice is the voice that
G　　　　　　D　　　　　　Am7   G/B   C2
　Is speaking words of love to me
　　　　　　　Am7   G/B   C2
How can it be?

Chorus:
　　G　　　　　C2
Awesome God Holy God
　　Em7　　　　　C2
I worship You in wonder
　　G　　　　　C2
Awesome God Holy God
　　Em7　　　　　　C2
As You draw near I 'm humbled
　　　　　Am7　　　　　C2
By Your majesty and the mystery
　　D　　　　　　　Em7   C/E   G/E   D
Of Your great love for me

Verse 2:
Your arms are the arms that
Hung shining stars in deepest space
Your arms are the arms that
Surround me in a warm embrace
Amazing grace

Taken from HOLY
Vineyard Music UK
VMUKCD06

YOUR VOICE IS LIKE THUNDER

Intimately, Reverently

David Gate

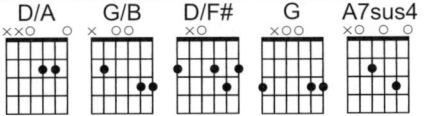

Verse 1:
    D/A   G/B
Your voice is like thunder
          D/A   G/B
Like the roar of the sea
          D/A   G/B
Yet You talk to us in whispers
            D/A   G/B
And You sing songs over me

Chorus:
D/F#   G   D/F#   G
Intimately, yet reverently
      D/F#   G   D/A   G
You call us, call us to praise
D/F#   G   D/F#   G
Intimately, yet reverently
      D/F#   G   D/A G/B
You call us, call us to praise

Verse 2:
    D/A   G/B
Your hands craft rivers and mountains
         D/A   G/B
And they hold stars in their place
     D/A   G/B
Yet still Your arms are open
     D/A   G/B
Our hearts You freely embrace

Bridge:
D/F#   G
With my face on the ground
A7sus4   G/B
And heart bowing down
D/F#   G
What else can I do
    A7sus4   G/B
But fall down and worship You

YOU'VE HAD MERCY ON ME

Shadows

Marc James

Chord diagrams: G C Am7 Dadd4 (5fr.) G/B C/E

Intro: G C Am7 C x2

Verse 1:
```
G              C        Am7    C
  You've had mercy on me
G    C            Am7    C
  According to Your love
G              C         Am7    C
  You've made a blind eye see
G          C       Am7    C
  Now I'm looking above
```

Pre-Chorus:
```
Dadd4           C
  Friend of the weak
         G/B    Dadd4
You lifted me up
                   C
From down on my knees
      G/B       Dadd4
Crying for Your love, You came to me
```

Chorus:
```
                     G    C    Dadd4
Now I'm singing of Your love
        C/E    Dadd4  G    C    Dadd4
In the shadows of Your wings
     C/E   Dadd4  G    C    Dadd4
I'm hiding in Your love
         C/E    Dadd4  C    G/B    Dadd4
In the shadows of Your wings
```

Verse 2:
You gave a new song to me
And You won me with Your blood
And though I'll never repay
This love You give to me
I want to show it to all the world

Taken from
BEAUTIFUL
Burn : UK
VMUKCD07

7 - The Unnoticed Worshipper

The conductor Leonard Bernstein was once asked, 'What is the most difficult instrument to play?' 'Second violin,' he replied, 'because everyone wants to be first violinist.'

Of course the first violin gets to play more interesting parts, and commands more attention. But, as Bernstein goes on to explain, 'It's hard to find someone who wants to play second violin and to do so with the same enthusiasm. But without the second violin, there is no harmony.'

There's a lesson here for all of us. So much of what we pay attention to in life happens on a stage of some kind. People like to be noticed, and our culture is in love with celebrity. Some will go to any length to make sure they get some attention. God, on the other hand, has a very different way of looking at things. He might watch the show, but He's much more concerned with what's going on backstage. We so often look at the appearance, but God goes straight to the heart. We become consumed with the public side of things, but God is always far more interested in the hidden and the private.

There's a great example of this in Luke 21:1-4. Jesus is watching the rich putting their gifts into the temple treasury, when a little act of hidden worship catches His eye. A poor widow walks up and puts in some tiny copper coins, worth almost nothing in the world's eyes. But Jesus declares, 'This poor widow has put in more than all the others'.

At first that sounds ridiculous, until we understand that Jesus is looking way beyond the coins themselves, right into her heart. He sees that these tiny coins, so gladly given, are all she has to live on. It's a costly, faithful offering of the heart, unnoticed by all around her, except for Jesus, who sees as heaven would. Unnoticed worshippers are not looking for attention from this world - their offerings are as private as possible. But because of what they bring, and the way they bring it, heaven is paying extra special attention. Unnoticed perhaps by those around them, they do not go unnoticed by the heart of God. Most examples in this book so far have been acts of worship carried out in public. But God seeks first devotion to Him in the hidden place - worship when no one else is watching.

The life of King David gives us some great insight into the balance of public and private in the heart of a worshipper. It seems pretty clear that David grew up knowing the Lord, no doubt offering up many passionate yet unnoticed acts of worship as he spent time alone tending sheep. In fact he was probably only 15 years old when Samuel described him to Saul as 'a man after [God's] own heart' (1 Samuel 13:14).

But then life gets a bit more complicated. David becomes the most well known worshipper in the whole of the land. From the Goliath incident onwards, he's involved in some very public acts of devotion. Women even start singing songs about him: 'Saul has slain his thousands, and David his tens of thousands' (1 Samuel 18:7). A few years later David becomes king.

In the midst of all this, the key for David is to try and maintain the heart of worship he had before life got complicated. In one sense it was easy then - for one thing, he could test his motives pretty simply. Every song he sang, and every prayer he prayed, was truly for an audience of one - no one else was around to witness his love for God in those lonely fields. Then he becomes a public figure, and from that time on his devotion is out in the open. The test was this: could he preserve that simple, pure heart of adoration in the midst of all the public things he became entrusted with?

And that's the test for all of us. I guess I'm talking more here to worship leaders and musicians than anyone else. The toughest test for our hearts doesn't come 'out in the fields' when there's no one else around. The really hard part begins when we start getting trusted with the public stuff. Maybe that's playing in the worship team at church, or wherever. God calls us to check ruthlessly the motives of our hearts. Do we still want to be unnoticed worshippers now that we're on a stage? Or is there a part of us that really wants to be a 'noticed' worshipper? Are we still happy to serve? Or is there even just a tiny part of us wanting to be served? Are our songs still aimed at an audience of one, or deep down are we starting to want wider acclaim? These are tough questions to face, but they're essential if we're going to stay faithful to the calling God has on our lives.

In the design of a boat, what's below the waterline must always outweigh what's above the waterline. Otherwise, the first sign of strong winds or waves and that boat will capsize. It's the same with our hearts. Things can look impressive on the outside - perhaps we've learnt a few cool guitar licks, or our voice seems stronger than ever. But God's infinitely more concerned with what's going on below the waterline. What are we like when no-one else can see us? How much do we throw ourselves into worship at church when we're not leading? Or, even more to the point, when someone else is leading worship in a style not quite to our taste?

And what's going through our minds when we lead? Are there little moments of self-congratulation when things are going well? Again, these are tough questions but so important if we're going to get this worship thing right, and really honour God. The key is to try and keep the public side of things outweighed by the private. As the late John Wimber taught, the real test in these days isn't going to be in the writing and producing of new and great worship music; the real test is going to be in the godliness of those who deliver it.

One trend in worship which increasingly worries me is the whole performance thing. It's been creeping up for years. Somehow we've got to a place where we'll even call worship events a 'gig' or 'concert'; the danger being that words like those throw us right off the scent of what worship really is. Too many times I've found myself in a meeting where I'm longing to engage with God while struggling to get past the impressive, yet ultimately distracting, show going on up the front. Some may argue that performance can be worship, and that's true. In one way, everything can be worship, if there's a good heart behind it. But performance is not necessarily a good way of leading worship. A worship leader needs as much as possible to be the unnoticed worshipper, simply encouraging the worship of God by setting an example for others to follow. To draw attention to ourselves in moments meant for a holy beholding is a pretty unbiblical approach. In fact, it's probably even a dangerous one.

Praise is a contradiction of pride. Pride says 'look at me', but praise longs for people to see Jesus. There's no room for showing off in the holy throne room. Picture it now: there we stand in the glorious presence of Almighty God; elders bowing as low as they can, and seraphs covering their faces. But there's one person - right in the middle of the whole thing - showing off a bit. A little dance routine, an over-the-top vocal, and just generally hamming it up. Ridiculous? Of course. And I've exaggerated to make a point, but I hope the point is clear. It wouldn't hurt to run everything we do in worship through that filter. The reality is that in the throne room of Almighty God, everyone's bowing as low as they can.

In the 1700's a Frenchman called Francois Fenelon wrote down some great advice for any worship leader: 'Make yourself little in the depths of your heart.' If we truly do this, our actions and attitudes will naturally follow through. If we make sure we're bowing low in our hearts, the chances are that the outward way we lead worship will be more appropriate too. Proverbs 25:6 sums it up: 'Do not exalt yourself in the king's presence.'

At a recent worship leaders' retreat, I believe God gave me a picture to illustrate this entrustment given to worship leaders. I saw a young man on a journey. He has been entrusted with the most beautiful jewel. Yet this treasure is not for him - he is on a mission to bring it before his king. So precious is the jewel that he hides it away as he travels along the road. Every now and then he stops at a town or village. And that's where the temptations start. It would be so easy to show his treasure off a bit, and let people marvel at this wonder he's been entrusted with. It would certainly bring him a lot of fame and favour. He could still take it to the king one day, but maybe have some fun along the way. Another temptation is to even settle down in that town, basking in his new-found popularity, and abandon the mission altogether. He could even sell the treasure. If he did, he'd never have to work again.

Every time he's around people, the enticements seem to grow stronger. And yet he remains faithful, and resists all these temptations, finally reaching the king's palace. Entering the throne room, with the treasure still intact, he looks up and sees the king. But more than that, he sees the king's pleasure; it is written all over his face.

Worship leaders, we're on a sacred journey. The cargo is precious, and the mission is vital. If we're to really see our King's pleasure in this whole worship music movement, then there are some narrow paths we need to cling to. At times it may seem more attractive to find pleasure from the people. Many of you have a lot of gifting and could certainly impress a lot of people. If you really wanted to, you could grab a whole lot of attention for yourself. But the challenge is this: to stay pure and true to the cause. Always keep in mind the end of the journey - the pleasure of the King over you, as you bring your unspoilt offering before Him, and Him alone.

In many ways this is a key time for worship leading. When things get exciting, it can be harder to maintain a purity. I came across one songbook recently called something like 'Today's 40 Most Powerful Worship Songs'. A shocking sign of the times. Who told them that? Was it God? How nice of Him to reveal His 40 favourites so that a book could be marketed effectively! I'm being extremely cheeky, and in all truth that same company has put out many wonderful resources, so I'm not picking on them. But it's a reminder to me. Let's test everything we do - every heart attitude, every way we lead worship, every resource we put out under the title of 'worship'.

It's a time to be on our guard - this is a sacred trust. Let's keep our worship pleasing to the Father, centred around the Son, and led by the Spirit, not the flesh.

Taken from 'The Unquenchable Worshipper'
Survivor Books 2001
Used by Permission

Index of Titles and First Lines

Authors' titles, where different from first lines, are shown in *italics*.

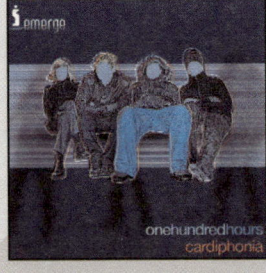
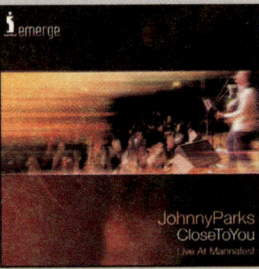

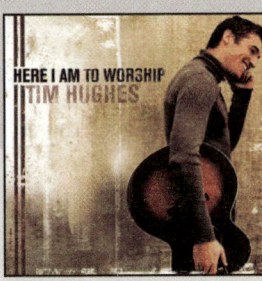

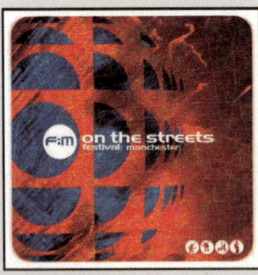